Taxcafe.co.uk Tax Guides

Capital Allowances

New Tax Saving Opportunities for
Business Owners & Property Investors

By Carl Bayley BSc ACA

Important Legal Notices:

Taxcafe®
TAX GUIDE – "Capital Allowances – New Tax Saving Opportunities for Business Owners & Property Investors"

Published by:
Taxcafe UK Limited
67 Milton Road
Kirkcaldy
KY1 1TL
United Kingdom
Tel: (01592) 560081

First Edition, January 2012

ISBN 978-1-907302-51-0

Disclaimer
Before reading or relying on the content of this Tax Guide, please read carefully the disclaimer on the last page which applies. If you have queries then please contact the publisher at team@taxcafe.co.uk.

Disclaimer

1. Please note that this Tax Guide is intended as general guidance only for individual readers and does NOT constitute accountancy, tax, investment or other professional advice. Neither Taxcafe UK Limited nor the author can accept any responsibility or liability for loss which may arise from reliance on information contained in this Tax Guide.

2. Please note that tax legislation, the law and practices by government and regulatory authorities (e.g. HM Revenue and Customs) are constantly changing. We therefore recommend that for accountancy, tax, investment or other professional advice, you consult a suitably qualified accountant, tax specialist, independent financial adviser, or other professional adviser. Please also note that your personal circumstances may vary from the general examples given in this Tax Guide and your professional adviser will be able to give specific advice based on your personal circumstances.

3. This Tax Guide covers UK taxation only and any references to 'tax' or 'taxation' in this Tax Guide, unless the contrary is expressly stated, refer to UK taxation only. Please note that references to the 'UK' do not include the Channel Islands or the Isle of Man. Foreign tax implications are beyond the scope of this Tax Guide.

4. Whilst in an effort to be helpful, this Tax Guide may refer to general guidance on matters other than UK taxation, Taxcafe UK Limited and the author are not expert in these matters and do not accept any responsibility or liability for loss which may arise from reliance on such information contained in this Tax Guide.

5. Please note that Taxcafe UK Limited has relied wholly on the expertise of the author in the preparation of the content of this Tax Guide. The author is not an employee of Taxcafe UK Limited but has been selected by Taxcafe UK Limited using reasonable care and skill to write the content of this Tax Guide.

About the Author

Carl Bayley is the author of a series of 'Plain English' tax guides designed specifically for the layman and the non-specialist. Carl's particular speciality is his ability to take the weird, complex and inexplicable world of taxation and set it out in the kind of clear, straightforward language that taxpayers themselves can understand. As he often says himself, "my job is to translate 'tax' into English".

Carl enjoys his role as a tax author, as he explains: "Writing these guides gives me the opportunity to use the skills and knowledge learned over more than twenty-five years in the tax profession for the benefit of a wider audience. The most satisfying part of my success as an author is the chance to give the average person the same standard of advice as the 'big guys' at a price which everyone can afford."

Carl takes the same approach when speaking on taxation, a role he frequently undertakes with great enthusiasm, including his highly acclaimed annual 'Budget Breakfast' for the Institute of Chartered Accountants.

In addition to being a recognised author and speaker on the subject, Carl has often spoken on taxation on radio and television, including the BBC's 'It's Your Money' programme and BBC Radio 2's Jeremy Vine Show.

Carl began his career as a Chartered Accountant in 1983 with one of the 'Big 4' accountancy firms. After qualifying as a double prize-winner, he immediately began specialising in taxation.

After honing his skills with several major international firms, Carl began the new millennium by launching his own tax and accounting practice, Bayley Miller Limited, through which he provides advice on a wide variety of taxation issues; especially property taxation and tax planning for small and medium-sized businesses.

Carl is a member of the governing Council of the Institute of Chartered Accountants in England and Wales and a former Chairman of ICAEW Scotland. He has co-organised the annual Peebles Tax Conference for the last ten years.

When he isn't working, Carl takes on the equally taxing challenges of hill walking and writing poetry and fiction – his Munro tally is now 57, but his first novel remains firmly in the planning stage!

Carl lives in Scotland with his partner Isabel and has four children.

Dedication

For the Past,

Firstly, I dedicate this book to the memory of those I have loved and lost:

First of all, to my beloved mother Diana – what would you think if you could see me now? The memory of your love warms me still. Thank you for making it all possible;

To my dear grandfather, Arthur - your wise words still come back to guide me; and to my loving grandmothers, Doris and Winifred;

Between you, you left me with nothing I could spend, but everything I need.

Also to my beloved friend and companion, Dawson, who waited so patiently for me to come home every night and who left me in the middle of our last walk together. Thank you for all those happy miles; I still miss you son.

For the Present,

Above all, I must dedicate this book to the person who stands, like a shining beacon, at the centre of every part of my life: Isabel, my 'life support system', whose unflinching support has seen me through the best and the worst. Whether anyone will ever call me a 'great man' I do not know, but I do know that I have a great woman behind me.

Without her help, support and encouragement, this book, and the others I have written, could never have been.

For the Future,

Finally, I also dedicate this book to four very special young people: Michelle, Louise, James and Robert.

I am so very proud of every one of you and I can only hope that I, in turn, will also be able to leave each of you with everything that you need.

Thanks

First and foremost, I must say an enormous thank you to Isabel: for all her help researching everything from obscure points of tax legislation to popular girls' names in Asia; for reading countless drafts; for making sure I stop to eat and sleep; for putting up with me when I'm under pressure and, most of all, for keeping me company into the 'wee small hours' on many a long and otherwise lonely night. I simply cannot ever thank her enough for everything that she does for me, but I intend to spend the rest of my life trying!

Thanks to the Taxcafe team, past and present, for their help in making these books far more successful than I could ever have dreamed.

I would like to thank my old friend and mentor, Peter Rayney, for his inspiration and for showing me that tax and humour can mix.

And last, but far from least, thanks to Ann for keeping us right!

C.B., Roxburghshire, January 2012

BUSINESS TAX SAVER

SPECIAL OFFER

If you like this tax guide...

You will also like *Business Tax Saver*...

Our monthly guide to BIG business tax savings

<u>You can try it now for FREE</u>

www.taxcafe.co.uk/businesstaxsaveroffer.html

Contents

Contents

Contents

Introduction

For as long as I can remember (which is now longer than I care to admit), there has been a constant process of change in the tax world. Tax regimes come and go with monotonous regularity. New tax reliefs arrive trumpeted as 'the next big thing' designed to stimulate growth in the economy, they flourish for a few years and then the Government wakes up to how much they are costing, panics, and abolishes them – only to replace them shortly afterwards with something even more complicated: yet another 'next big thing'.

Nevertheless, whilst this process of constant change is nothing new, the arrival of the new Coalition Government in May 2010 seemed to herald a new era of even greater and more rapid change than ever before.

Whether by coincidence or design, a significant part of this change is currently focussed on capital allowances.

First of all, the amounts of capital allowances currently available are due to be drastically reduced with effect from April 2012. Once these reductions are in place, obtaining tax relief for some business investments will take decades instead of being available immediately in the year of investment, as it is now.

The April 2012 changes bring even greater dangers in the shape of transitional rules which carry some unexpected pitfalls. Businesses with accounting periods which span the date of the changes need to be particularly wary, as the date on which they incur qualifying expenditure can make an enormous difference to the amount of allowances available.

On top of these changes, there are further proposals to implement strict new time limits and other restrictions on capital allowances claims for fixtures within commercial property, qualifying furnished holiday lettings, and other properties such as some 'Houses in Multiple Occupation' (often known as 'HMOs').

The proposals regarding capital allowances on fixtures could mean that millions of pounds of unclaimed allowances are lost forever.

It is essential that businesses and property investors act soon to preserve the availability of these valuable allowances.

Other recent changes are also having an impact, including HM Revenue and Customs changing their mind about capital allowances claims for fixtures and equipment within HMOs – twice! And in quick succession!

All these changes give rise to both opportunities for well-advised businesses and property investors to maximise the benefits of the capital allowances regime, as well as traps and pitfalls for the unwary and ill-informed.

And that's why I have written this guide – so that you can fall into the 'well-advised' category and make sure that you don't miss out on any of the allowances that you're rightfully entitled to.

Scope of this Guide

This guide covers the UK capital allowances regime only. It is aimed purely at individuals, companies, and other entities carrying on qualifying activities, whether in the UK or elsewhere, for the purposes of UK capital allowances. The UK does not include the Channel Islands or the Isle of Man.

All foreign taxation implications are beyond the scope of this guide.

The reader must also bear in mind the general nature of this guide. Individual circumstances vary and the tax implications of an individual's actions will vary with them. For this reason, it is always vital to get professional advice before undertaking any tax planning or other transactions which may have tax implications. The author cannot accept any responsibility for any loss which may arise as a consequence of any action taken, or any decision to refrain from action taken, as a result of reading this guide.

A Word about the Examples in this Guide

This guide is illustrated throughout by a number of examples.

Unless specifically stated to the contrary, all persons described in the examples in this guide are UK resident, ordinarily resident and domiciled for tax purposes.

In preparing the examples in this guide, we have assumed that the UK tax regime will remain unchanged in the future except to the extent of any announcements already made at the time of publication.

It is, however, important to understand that some proposals and announcements are not yet law and may undergo some alteration before they are formally enacted.

Furthermore, if there is one thing which we can predict with any certainty, it is the fact that change **will** occur. The reader must bear this in mind when reviewing the results of our examples.

All persons described in the examples in this guide are entirely fictional characters created specifically for the purposes of this guide. Any similarities to actual persons, living or dead, or to fictional characters created by any other author, are entirely coincidental.

Chapter 1

The Current Capital Allowances Regime

1.1 WHAT ARE CAPITAL ALLOWANCES?

One of the basic fundamental principles in UK taxation is the 'capital or revenue' question.

When a business, or other qualifying entity, incurs any item of expenditure, we have to consider whether that item is 'capital' or 'revenue'.

Revenue expenditure is the type of expenditure which we all incur, on a day-to-day basis, to keep our business going: like paying an electricity bill, buying stationery, paying staff wages, purchasing stock, travel and subsistence costs, etc, etc.

All this expenditure just keeps the business going – it does not provide us with any sort of asset.

But, from time to time, we also incur another type of expenditure – capital expenditure on assets which we will use in our business for some time to come, like furniture, computers, vehicles, property and equipment.

We cannot claim a direct deduction for the cost of these 'capital' items, but the tax system does recognise that there is a legitimate business expense involved (in some cases anyway).

That's where capital allowances come in: a tax deduction to cover the cost of capital items which we use in our business.

However, as we shall see, this is just the beginning, because there is a whole regime-full of rules and regulations covering who can claim capital allowances, how much, and on what expenditure. And that regime is in the midst of several very important changes!

1.2 WHO CAN CLAIM CAPITAL ALLOWANCES?

Before any entity can claim anything under the UK capital allowances regime, it must be carrying on a qualifying activity and be subject to UK tax. If you're not subject to UK tax, there's not much point thinking about UK capital allowances!

The qualifying activities for the purposes of capital allowances are:

- Trades and professions
- 'Ordinary' UK property businesses
- 'Ordinary' overseas property businesses
- Furnished holiday letting in the UK
- Furnished holiday letting elsewhere in the European Economic Area (see Appendix B)

Each of these activities must be dealt with completely separately for capital allowances purposes, even when carried on by the same entity.

An 'ordinary' property business means any form of property letting other than furnished holiday letting. It covers both residential property businesses and commercial property letting.

Hence, residential property businesses can, in principle, claim capital allowances. However, there are major restrictions on the type of expenditure on which capital allowances may be claimed in a residential property business. I will cover this point in more detail in Section 2.10.

Any entity carrying on any of the above activities may claim capital allowances, including: individuals, companies, partnerships (including limited liability partnerships), and trusts.

Most of these entities are subject to much the same rules for capital allowances purposes, although there are slightly different rules for companies: mostly based around the fact that the 'financial year' for company taxation starts on 1st April, whereas the tax year applying to all other entities starts on 6th April.

1.3   WHAT CAPITAL ALLOWANCES ARE AVAILABLE?

In the next few sections, I am going to summarise the capital allowances currently available to any business entity with an accounting period which ends before:

- 1st April 2012 in the case of companies, and
- 6th April 2012 in the case of other business entities

I will focus predominantly on the current regime. Other important changes took place each year in April 2008, 2009 and 2010. Where these impact on current expenditure or current capital allowances claims, I will cover them as appropriate.

For the rest of this chapter, I will also be focussing purely on 'plant and machinery allowances', as these are the allowances which are undergoing all of the major changes which I discussed in the Introduction.

The term 'plant and machinery' covers qualifying plant, machinery, vehicles, furniture, fixtures, fittings, computers and other equipment used in a business.

It also covers cars which are wholly or partly used in a qualifying business activity, or which are provided to employees who work in such a business. However, cars are subject to a different capital allowances regime to other qualifying 'plant and machinery', so we will look at them separately (see Sections 1.8 to 1.10).

Precisely what qualifies as 'plant and machinery' for capital allowances purposes depends to a large extent on the nature of the business, so we will look at this further in Chapter 2.

In Chapter 3, I will also take a brief look at some other important capital allowances which are currently available. The importance of some of these will increase significantly following the proposed changes to plant and machinery allowances in April 2012.

1.4 THE ANNUAL INVESTMENT ALLOWANCE

The annual investment allowance provides 100% tax relief for qualifying expenditure on plant and machinery up to the maximum amount of the allowance available for each accounting period.

The allowance is available to sole traders, partnerships and companies alike. Some restrictions apply to companies in groups and also to other companies or businesses which are closely related to each other (see Section 1.12).

The maximum amount of annual investment allowance available depends on the business's accounting period, as follows:

Companies
Accounting periods falling into the period:
- 1st April 2008 to 31st March 2010:   £50,000
- 1st April 2010 to 31st March 2012:   £100,000
- 1st April 2012 onwards: £25,000

Other Businesses
Accounting periods falling into the period:
- 6th April 2008 to 5th April 2010:   £50,000
- 6th April 2010 to 5th April 2012:   £100,000
- 6th April 2012 onwards: £25,000

Transitional rules apply to determine the maximum amount of annual investment allowance available where an accounting period straddles one of the above dates. The transitional rules applying to business accounting periods straddling 1st or 6th April 2012 are a major cause for concern and we will be looking at these in detail in Chapter 7.

The annual investment allowance is also restricted where there is an accounting period of less than twelve months' duration. This will often apply to a new business's first accounting period.

The annual investment allowance is available to most business entities, but it is not available to a 'mixed partnership': where one or more members of the partnership are a company.

1.5   FIRST YEAR ALLOWANCES

Qualifying capital expenditure on plant and machinery in excess of the annual investment allowance incurred between 6th April 2009 and 5th April 2010 (between 1st April 2009 and 31st March 2010 for companies) was eligible for a first year allowance of 40%.

Most expenditure incurred after April 2010 is not eligible for any first year allowances. However, there are a few notable exceptions where 'enhanced capital allowances' of 100% are available immediately for the accounting period in which the expenditure is incurred. In each case, the enhanced capital allowances are available in addition to the annual investment allowance. In other words, the enhanced capital allowances claim does not need to be counted towards the business's maximum annual investment allowance for the accounting period.

Energy-Saving Plant & Machinery

Various qualifying energy-saving equipment is eligible for a 100% first year allowance. The equipment needs to be within one of the 'designated technologies' on the 'Energy Technology List' and must also meet various other qualifying criteria. The Energy Technology List and the associated criteria are revised regularly. The list currently includes:

- Combined heat and power
- Boilers and boiler add-ons
- Lighting
- Pipe insulation
- Motors and variable speed drives
- Refrigeration equipment
- Heat pumps for space heating
- Radiant and warm air heaters
- Compressed air equipment
- Automatic monitoring and targeting equipment
- Air-to-air energy recovery equipment
- Compact heat exchangers
- Heating, ventilation and air-conditioning zone controls
- Uninterruptible power supplies
- High speed hand air dryers
- Solar thermal systems

This allowance is available to businesses of all sizes and applies to qualifying expenditure incurred at any time (provided it meets the qualifying criteria applying at the relevant time).

For further details see www.etl.decc.gov.uk

Environmentally Beneficial Plant & Machinery

Certain water technologies also qualify for a 100% first year allowance. Again, there are no restrictions on the size of the business and the expenditure has to meet the qualifying criteria applying at the relevant time. The technologies currently eligible for the allowance are:

- Cleaning in-place equipment
- Efficient showers
- Efficient taps
- Efficient toilets
- Efficient washing machines
- Flow controllers
- Leakage detection equipment
- Meters and monitoring equipment
- Rainwater harvesting equipment
- Small-scale slurry and sludge dewatering equipment
- Vehicle wash water reclaim units
- Water efficient industrial cleaning equipment
- Water management equipment for mechanical seals
- Wastewater recovery and re-use systems

For further details see www.envirowise.wrap.org.uk

Refuelling Equipment for 'Green' Vehicles

Expenditure on refuelling equipment for natural gas, hydrogen or biogas vehicles incurred before 1st April 2013 is eligible for a 100% first year allowance.

Research & Development

Plant and machinery used in qualifying research and development activities qualifies for a 100% first year allowance.

Enterprise Zones

The Government has announced that enhanced capital allowances of 100% are to be made available for qualifying expenditure on plant and machinery incurred between 1st April 2012 and 31st March 2017 for use within Assisted Areas lying within new Enterprise Zones, including:

- Black Country
- Humber
- Liverpool
- North Eastern
- Sheffield
- Tees Valley

'Assisted Areas' are defined by the Assisted Areas Order SI 2007/107, which is available online.

Remember, the expenditure must be on assets for use within both an Assisted Area and an Enterprise Zone. In other words, the location where the asset will be used must lie within both.

Furthermore, the asset must not be used outside a relevant qualifying assisted area for at least five years.

This particular allowance is only available to companies and only for new investment and not for replacement assets. It is also only available to trading companies and certain industries are excluded.

There is an overall limit for qualifying expenditure of €125 million per project and expenditure qualifying for a grant, or even just taken into account for the purposes of a grant, is excluded.

Despite all these restrictions, the Government expects this new relief to cost them almost £100 million, so someone has to benefit!

Enhanced Capital Allowances Restrictions

All of the enhanced capital allowances discussed above are available on new assets only (i.e. not on used or second-hand items).

The assets must not be held for leasing. This can sometimes include assets provided by landlords within rented property, although certain 'background' fixtures may still qualify (see Section 2.8 for further details).

Carry Forward of Expenditure

Where first year allowances of less than 100% are available, the unclaimed balance of any qualifying capital expenditure is carried forward to the next accounting period. It will then attract writing down allowances at the appropriate rate.

1.6   WRITING DOWN ALLOWANCES

Any remaining expenditure on qualifying plant and machinery which is not covered by the annual investment allowance and does not qualify for first year allowances is eligible for writing down allowances.

The rate of writing down allowances available is dependent on the type of expenditure involved. The current rates applying to accounting periods ending before 6th April 2012 (or 1st April 2012 for companies) are:

- 10% for items falling into the 'Special Rate Pool'
- 20% for other qualifying plant and machinery

Most plant and machinery qualifies for the 20% rate and falls into the 'General Pool' (sometimes also known as the 'Main Pool'). We will look at the items falling into the special rate pool in Section 1.7.

Transitional rules apply to accounting periods spanning the date of change on 1st or 6th April 2012. In essence, these rules will give rise to writing down allowance rates of somewhere between 18% and 20% for the general pool and somewhere between 8% and

10% for the special rate pool. We will look at these transitional rules in further detail in Section 7.3.

Expenditure qualifying for writing down allowances is pooled together with the unrelieved balance of qualifying expenditure brought forward from the previous accounting period within the same pool (i.e. either the 'general pool' or the 'special rate pool').

The writing down allowance at the appropriate rate is then calculated on the total balance in the relevant pool.

The remaining balance of expenditure is then carried forward and the appropriate percentage of that balance may be claimed in the next accounting period. And so on.

However, where the balance in either pool reduces to less than £1,000, the full balance may then be claimed immediately.

Example

During the year ended 31st December 2011, Aman spent £101,800 on qualifying plant and machinery for her trading business.

The first £100,000 of her expenditure is covered by the annual investment allowance (see Section 1.4) and she therefore obtains immediate tax relief for the whole of this sum.

The remaining £1,800 is eligible for a writing down allowance of £360 (20%). The 'unrelieved' balance of this expenditure, £1,440, is carried forward to the year ending 31st December 2012.

Aman's total capital allowances for the year ending 31st December 2011 are:

Annual investment allowance:	*£100,000*
Writing down allowance:	*£360*
Total allowances claimed:	*£100,360*

All of Aman's qualifying capital expenditure in each of the next three years is fully relieved by the annual investment allowance.

In the year ending 31st December 2012, she is also able to claim an 18.5% writing down allowance (under the transitional rules - Section

7.3) on the £1,440 balance of unrelieved expenditure brought forward from the previous year: i.e. £266.

A balance of £1,174 is then carried forward again to the year ending 31st December 2013 when Aman is able to claim a writing down allowance of 18%, or £211.

This leaves a balance of £963 carried forward. As this is less than £1,000, Aman will be able to claim this balance in full in the year ending 31st December 2014.

The rates of writing down allowances claimed by Aman in future years are explained in Sections 5.2 and 7.3.

Note that, for the sake of illustration, I have assumed throughout this example that Aman did not have any balance on her general pool brought forward from the year ended 31st December 2010.

Note also that, if Aman had spent more than the maximum amount of the annual investment allowance on qualifying plant and machinery in any future year, the excess would be added to the general pool and the process of claiming 18% of the remainder each year would be further prolonged, perhaps indefinitely!

1.7   THE SPECIAL RATE POOL

Certain types of expenditure must be allocated to a 'special rate pool' instead of the general pool. These include:

- Certain defined categories of 'integral features' (see Section 2.5).
- Expenditure of £100,000 or more on plant and machinery with an anticipated working life of 25 years or more.
- Expenditure on thermal insulation of an existing building used in a qualifying trade.

Expenditure in the special rate pool is currently eligible for writing down allowances at just 10%, instead of the usual 20%, and was ineligible for the temporary first year allowances applying in 2009/10 (see Section 1.5).

It is worth noting, however, that the annual investment allowance may be allocated to any such expenditure in preference to expenditure qualifying for the normal rate of writing down allowance.

This is particularly relevant to trading businesses purchasing their own business premises and to property investors letting out commercial property or qualifying furnished holiday accommodation.

1.8 CAPITAL ALLOWANCES ON CARS

Plant and machinery allowances are available on motor vehicles used in a qualifying business.

Vans and other commercial vehicles are generally eligible for the same allowances as other plant and machinery, as described in the preceding sections.

Cars, however, are not generally eligible for the annual investment allowance or for first year allowances: but they do have their own system of writing down allowances.

There are now effectively two different capital allowances regimes for cars which are used in a business. These two regimes apply to:

    a)   Company cars and other cars with no private use.
    b)   Business owner's cars with some private use.

The first regime is actually broader than one might think and applies to:

    i)   Cars provided to employees,
    ii)   Cars owned by a company, and
    iii) Other cars which are wholly used for business purposes.

Cars falling under heading (iii) are pretty rare as this means that the car is owned and used by the owner of the business and there is absolutely no private use of the vehicle. In over twenty-five years as a tax adviser, I have never encountered such a car.

Cars subject to the first regime are therefore generally referred to as 'company cars', whether owned by a company or not. We will look at the capital allowances regime for these cars in Section 1.9. Note that the 'company car' regime includes cars provided to company directors by their company.

In Section 1.10, I will look at the second regime: i.e. cars owned and used by the business owner themselves which have some element of private use.

In both cases, the treatment varies according to whether the car was purchased before or after 6th April 2009 (1st April 2009 for companies). In the sections which follow, I will be looking purely at the treatment of cars purchased on or after those dates.

As cars do not generally qualify for the annual investment allowance, the changes proposed for April 2012 will not have such a big impact on capital allowances claims for cars as they will for other assets. Nonetheless, as we will see in Section 5.3, even the apparently quite small reductions in the rates of writing down allowances available can have a pretty significant impact.

1.9 COMPANY CARS

The capital allowances available on company cars purchased after 31st March 2009 (5th April 2009 where the business is not a company) depend on the car's CO_2 emissions level.

Cars with CO_2 emissions in excess of 160g/km are added to the special rate pool and would currently attract writing down allowances of 10%.

Cars with CO_2 emissions of more than 110g/km but not over 160g/km are added to the general pool and would currently attract writing down allowances of 20%.

Cars with CO_2 emissions of 110g/km or less attract a 100% first year allowance. However, this will cease to apply for cars purchased after 31st March 2013.

The key point to bear in mind about company cars purchased from April 2009 onwards (or at least those with CO_2 emissions over 110g/km anyway) is that there is generally no longer any balancing allowance on a sale of the car. The remaining balance of expenditure just attracts writing down allowances and it may therefore take many years to obtain full tax relief for the economic cost of the car.

See Section 1.10 for an explanation of balancing allowances.

1.10 BUSINESS OWNERS' CARS

Cars owned by a business owner and used for business purposes, which also have some element of private use, must each be put in their own individual pool for capital allowances purposes.

For cars purchased after 5th April 2009, the rate of writing down allowances available depends on the car's CO_2 emissions.

The actual rates of the allowance are the same as for company cars (see Section 1.9), but there are two key differences to be aware of:

i) The allowances claimed must be restricted to reflect the element of private use of the car.
ii) Balancing allowances or charges will arise on a sale (or other disposal) of the car.

For example, a car purchased during an accounting year ending before 6th April 2012 for £20,000, which has 170g/km of CO_2 emissions and 75% private use, will be eligible for an allowance of £500 (10% x £20,000 = £2,000 less 75%).

A car purchased during an accounting year ending before 6th April 2012 for £10,000 which has 150g/km of CO_2 emissions and 60% private use will be eligible for an allowance of £800 (20% x £10,000 = £2,000 less 60%).

Note that the unrelieved balance of expenditure to be carried forward to the next period is calculated before the deduction in respect of private use.

Balancing Allowances and Charges

When a car with private use is sold (or otherwise disposed of), a balancing allowance, or charge, will arise, reflecting the difference between the sale price (or other disposal proceeds) and the unrelieved balance of expenditure.

A balancing allowance, like any other capital allowance, is a deduction from taxable income. A balancing charge is added to taxable income.

Balancing allowances and charges on cars with private use are subject to the same restriction in respect of private use as writing down allowances.

Summary of Capital Allowances on Cars with Private Use

To summarise the position, let's look at an example.

Example

In February 2012, Lewis buys a car for £20,000 and uses it 30% for his business and 70% privately. The car has 142g/km of CO_2 emissions.

In his accounts for the year to 31st March 2012, Lewis claims a writing down allowance of £1,200 (£20,000 x 20% x 30%). However, the unrelieved balance carried forward to the next year is just £16,000 (£20,000 – 20%).

For the year ending 31st March 2013, Lewis is able to claim a writing down allowance of £865 (£16,000 x 18.03% x 30%). The unrelieved balance carried forward this time is £13,115 (£16,000 – 18.03%).

In February 2014, Lewis sells the car for £12,000. This gives rise to a balancing allowance of £335 (£13,115 - £12,000 = £1,115 x 30%).

See Sections 5.3 and 7.3 for an explanation of the rates of writing down allowances available on Lewis's car in future years.

Note that, if Lewis had sold the car for more than £13,115 (the unrelieved balance of expenditure), he would have been subject to a balancing charge. The charge in this case would have been 30% of the excess of the sale price over £13,115.

Mileage Claims

Business owners claiming the fixed mileage rate for their business travel (45p per mile for the first 10,000 miles per year – or 40p per mile before 6th April 2011 – and 25p per mile for any excess) cannot also claim capital allowances on their car.

1.11 OTHER ASSETS WITH PRIVATE USE

The capital allowances regime for business owners' cars is echoed to some extent in the case of other assets with an element of private use.

Where an asset is purchased and used by a business owner, capital allowances remain available but, as with cars, a suitable deduction must be made in respect of the private use of the asset.

All such assets must also each be placed in their own capital allowances pool, or 'puddle', as I like to call them.

The current rate of writing down allowances on these 'puddles' will be either 10% or 20%, as appropriate, less the deduction for private use. (Subject to the same transitional rules where the accounting period spans 1st or 6th April 2012 as for the general pool and special rate pool – see Section 7.3.)

As with cars, the unrelieved balance on the 'puddle' carried forward to the next period is calculated before the deduction for private use.

The great advantage (or occasional disadvantage) of the 'puddle' is that a balancing allowance (or charge) will arise when each asset is disposed of. These balancing allowances or charges are calculated in exactly the same way as for a car with private use, as explained in Section 1.10.

Balances under £1,000 in 'puddles' cannot be written off like similar small balances in the general or special rate pools.

The annual investment allowance is available on assets (other than cars) with an element of private use. The allowance must, however, be restricted to reflect the private use, so the annual investment allowance should be allocated to other expenditure first whenever possible.

Assets purchased for a business proprietor's own use can only attract allowances if genuinely used in the business.

1.12 RELATED BUSINESSES

Related businesses under common control must share one single annual investment allowance between them. In other words, a total annual investment allowance equal to the amount described in Section 1.4 for the appropriate period (subject to the transitional rules in Chapter 7) is available to all of the related businesses taken together.

The related businesses may allocate the annual investment allowance between them in whatever proportions they wish.

Fortunately, the 'related business' rules have been drawn up with a very 'light touch' and are designed to ensure that the vast majority of businesses will be entitled to a full annual investment allowance.

Generally speaking, the rules only come into play when the businesses are **both** deemed to be 'related' (as explained below) **and** under common control.

However, a group of companies (i.e. the parent holding company and all its subsidiaries) will always be treated as all being related and will therefore have to share a single annual investment allowance.

Common Control

To test whether two or more companies or other businesses are under common control, we simply look to see whether they are controlled by the same person or the same group of two or more persons.

A person, or group of persons, is generally deemed to control a company or a business whenever they are entitled to more than half of the profits, more than half of the assets, or more than half of the voting rights (in the case of a company).

Obviously, a sole trader controls all of the businesses which they run.

One or more partners may control a partnership, depending on the way in which the profits are split and the rights the partners have to the partnership assets.

One or more shareholders may control a company, generally depending on voting rights.

There are no 'connected persons' rules for the purposes of the annual investment allowance, so we do not need to consider businesses or companies controlled by a business owner's spouse, civil partner or other close family: only other businesses or companies controlled by the same individual or the same group of individuals.

For example, if a married couple each own their own separate business, these businesses are not under 'common control' for the purposes of the annual investment allowance. However, if the same couple owns two businesses in equal 50/50 shares as a partnership, then those businesses are under 'common control' and may have to share a single annual investment allowance if they are also deemed to be 'related', as explained below.

The Meaning of 'Related'

Broadly speaking, companies and other businesses are only 'related' with each other if they are either carried on from the same premises or carry on similar activities.

Whether two activities are regarded as similar is taken at a very broad level, so that even any vaguely similar businesses are likely to be regarded as 'related'. (The precise definition is based on the 'NACE' classifications established by Regulation (EC) 1893/2006 of the European Parliament)

For the purposes of the annual investment allowance, a company can only ever be considered to be 'related' to another company; and an unincorporated business (i.e. a sole trader or partnership) can only ever be considered to be 'related' to another unincorporated business.

Tax Tip

Companies and unincorporated businesses (sole trades and partnerships) never have to share an annual investment allowance with each other.

Example

John has a large number of business interests, as follows:

- *A sole trade as a concert promoter*
- *A 75% share in the assets and income of Winston & Co. LLP, a music publishing partnership. (Winston & Co. LLP also owns and rents out several commercial properties)*
- *51% of the voting shares in Ono Limited, a company which manufactures CDs and DVDs*
- *25% of the voting shares in Yoko Limited, another concert promotion company (John's wife Cynthia owns the other 75% of the voting shares)*
- *Joint ownership with his wife Cynthia of several commercial rental properties*

Cynthia also operates her own separate music publishing business as a sole trader.

All of these businesses are run from the same premises except that Cynthia runs the couple's joint commercial property letting business from home.

A single annual investment allowance must be shared between:

- *John's sole trade as a concert promoter*
- *Winston & Co. LLP's music publishing business*
- *Winston & Co. LLP's commercial property letting business*
- *John's own share of his joint commercial property letting business with Cynthia*

The first three businesses are under common control and share the same premises.

Where rental property is owned jointly, each joint owner has their own property letting business. John's share is under common control with, and is the same activity as, Winston & Co. LLP's commercial property letting business.

Ono Limited and Yoko Limited are each entitled to their own annual investment allowance. The fact that John's wife Cynthia controls Yoko Limited is immaterial.

Cynthia is also entitled to her own annual investment allowance in respect of her own music publishing business and is also entitled to a further annual investment allowance in respect of her share of the couple's joint commercial property letting business. Although these businesses are under common control, they neither share the same premises, nor are they classed as similar activities.

Multiple Allowances (But Not For Companies)

An interesting point to note here is that, although a company can only ever have one annual investment allowance (at most), no matter how many qualifying activities it carries on, individuals or partnerships may have more than one annual investment allowance. In fact, individuals and partnerships are entitled to a different annual investment allowance for each separate qualifying activity they carry on, as long as the activities are carried on from different premises and are not regarded as 'similar'.

Multiple Allowances For Landlords

As we saw in the example, landlords owning property jointly (but not as a partnership) each have their own property business for tax purposes. Each of these businesses will be entitled to its own annual investment allowance, as they are not under 'common control'.

This means that a couple (or any other pair of individuals) owning property jointly can benefit from a double annual investment allowance.

In fact, it is even possible for any two people to obtain a quadruple annual investment allowance by owning a property jointly between:

- The first individual,
- The second individual,
- A company controlled by the first individual, and
- A company controlled by the second individual

Note, however, that these two companies would be regarded as 'connected' for other tax purposes, which might lead to increased Corporation Tax liabilities in some cases.

1.13 ADDITIONAL POINTS

Both the annual investment allowance and all writing down allowances, including allowances on cars, are restricted where there is an accounting period of less than twelve months.

Neither the annual investment allowance nor any first year allowances are available on used assets which a business owner introduces into the business. Assets acquired from connected persons (see Appendix C) are also ineligible for both the annual investment allowance and first year allowances. Writing down allowances generally remain available in these cases, however.

None of the usual allowances are available in the final accounting period when a business ceases. A balancing allowance or charge will apply instead, based on the difference between the unrelieved balance of expenditure and the total value of the remaining business assets at the date of cessation.

Assets bought on hire purchase continue to be eligible for capital allowances as normal but must be brought into use in the business before the end of the accounting period.

Subject to the above points (and the transitional rules set out in Section 7.2), the full allowance due is available on any business asset purchased part-way through an accounting period – even on the last day.

Chapter 2

What Is Plant and Machinery?

2.1 QUALIFYING ACTIVITIES

In Section 1.2 we looked at the various 'qualifying activities' for the purposes of capital allowances.

Each of these activities must be treated as a separate business for capital allowances purposes.

However, the items qualifying as plant and machinery are generally much the same for each activity. With one notable exception: landlords renting out residential property.

As so often in tax, this exception has an exception itself: furnished holiday lettings are treated much the same as commercial property for capital allowances purposes.

We will look at the position for landlords renting out all types of property later in this chapter (see Sections 2.8 to 2.12, which are then summarised in Section 2.13).

Before that, however, let's look at what qualifies as plant and machinery in other cases: namely, assets purchased for use in a trade or profession.

2.2 TRADES AND PROFESSIONS

Most businesses other than property rental or stock market investment are classed as a trade or profession. For most tax purposes, there is really no difference in treatment between a trade and a profession and certainly not for capital allowances. Hence, for the rest of this chapter, I will just refer to trades.

What qualifies as plant and machinery depends to a large extent on the nature of the trade. A hotel with a piano lounge could claim capital allowances on a piano, but, for a piano manufacturer, the completed pianos which it holds are stock, their cost is deducted from their sale proceeds, and no capital allowances are available.

Hence, before anything can qualify for capital allowances, it has to be a long-term asset of the business. 'Long-term' is generally taken to mean that it has a useful working life of two years or more.

The things which the business sells cannot qualify for capital allowances because they are stock and not capital assets.

The most important cases in point are property developers who cannot claim any capital allowances on any assets within their development properties. However, assets within their own business premises would qualify in the same way as any other trading business (we will be looking at plant and machinery within property in Sections 2.4 and 2.5).

Consumable items with a working life of less than two years will not qualify for capital allowances as they will simply be charged in the business's accounts as they are purchased or consumed.

Similarly, repairs expenditure does not generally qualify for capital allowances because it is again charged in the business's accounts as it is incurred. There is, however, an exception in the case of major repairs to assets which are classed as 'integral features' and we will look at this in Section 2.6.

2.3   BUT WHAT IS PLANT AND MACHINERY?

Having eliminated items in stock and consumables and repairs expenditure, we are still left with the question of what actually is plant and machinery.

Most people do not have any difficulty with the word 'machinery' but 'plant' is a rather more elusive concept.

The best that I can come up with is to say that 'plant' is any other kind of tangible moveable asset. (Tangible being anything with a real physical existence: i.e. you can touch it!)

This is a reasonably good definition, but it does not cover fixtures or computer software, both of which may qualify as plant and machinery for capital allowances purposes. (We will look at fixtures in detail in Section 2.4.) So, apart from fixtures and computer software, what we are generally talking about is tangible moveable assets which are used in the qualifying activity.

It would be next to impossible to produce an exhaustive list of everything which may qualify as plant and machinery, but some of the most common items are:

- Machinery
- Large tools (small tools are usually treated as consumable items)
- Furniture
- Electrical equipment (televisions, radios, vacuum cleaners, kettles, etc)
- Computers, printers, etc
- Telephones and other telecommunications equipment
- Other office equipment
- Cars (see Sections 1.8 to 1.10)
- Vans and other commercial vehicles
- Fixtures and fittings (see Sections 2.4 and 2.5)
- Computer software with a useful life of over two years

2.4   CAPITAL ALLOWANCES ON PROPERTY

Buildings do not generally qualify as plant and machinery for capital allowances purposes. However, many items within a property may qualify.

The tax legislation contains a specific list of items within buildings and other structures which may qualify as plant and machinery. These are:

- Integral features (see Section 2.5)
- Machinery
- Manufacturing and processing equipment
- Storage and display equipment and checkouts
- White goods (cookers, refrigerators, dishwashers, etc.)
- Sinks, baths, showers and sanitary ware
- Furniture & furnishings (curtains, blinds, rugs, etc)
- Hoists

- Computer, telecommunication and surveillance systems, including wiring and other links
- Refrigeration or cooling equipment
- Fire alarms, sprinklers, and other fire-fighting equipment
- Burglar alarm systems
- Strong rooms (in banks, etc) & safes
- Moveable partitioning (if intended to be moved in the course of the trade)
- Decorative assets provided for the enjoyment of the public (in hotels, restaurants, and other similar establishments)
- Swimming pools
- Cold Stores

Certain further items may also qualify as plant and machinery where they are specialised items specific to the needs of the trade being carried out in the property:

- Gas pipes and other items comprised in gas systems
- Sewerage pipes, etc.
- Sound insulation

In addition to items within buildings, there are a few types of buildings and structures which qualify as plant and machinery in their own right, these are:

- Advertising hoardings, signs and displays
- Automated glasshouses
- Caravans used for holiday lettings
- Buildings for testing aircraft engines
- Moveable buildings (if intended to be moved in the course of the trade)
- Dry docks
- Jetties
- Pipelines & underground ducts (used by utility providers)
- Floodlight towers
- Reservoirs (for water supplies)
- Silos, storage tanks, slurry pits & silage clamps
- Fish tanks & fish ponds
- Rails, sleepers & ballast
- Amusement park rides
- Zoo cages

These items will also still qualify if housed within a larger building. Similarly, items listed earlier in this section would qualify if they were a separate structure.

The cost of any alterations to land or buildings which are specifically required purely in order to install qualifying plant and machinery will also qualify for capital allowances. This also extends to any structures which are specifically required purely for the same purpose.

Further provisions may also provide capital allowances on building expenditure in certain special cases. These include:

- Expenditure on safety at sports grounds (incurred before 1st April 2013 for companies and before 6th April 2013 in other cases)
- Personal security expenditure where a 'special threat' exists
- Qualifying film expenditure

Testing the Boundaries

In 2008, the well-known pub company, JD Wetherspoon Ltd, tested some of the boundaries for qualifying plant and machinery in buildings. The results of the case heard by the Special Commissioners (a type of Court equivalent to the current tax tribunals) are useful in telling us where some of those boundaries lie.

Firstly, the company argued that wood panelling qualified as plant on the basis that it was a 'decorative asset provided for the enjoyment of the public'. They lost: the Commissioners held that the panelling became part of the premises and could not qualify.

The Commissioners also held that kitchen walls could not be regarded as 'alterations to land or buildings specifically required in order to install qualifying plant and machinery'. Although the walls were needed to enable a cooker to function, they were merely incidental to the installation of the qualifying plant. The Commissioners felt that allowing a claim for the walls would be stretching the relevant provision a little too far, as the walls were part of the creation of the kitchen and did not have sufficient link with the installation of the equipment to qualify.

Wipe-clean tiling on the kitchen walls also failed to qualify as plant – it was part of the wall, the Commissioners said.

The company did, however, succeed in its capital allowances claim for the cost of partitions and doors to individual toilets, as the Commissioners agreed that these were required for the proper use of the toilets. This seems a little odd, as it is hard to see how the toilet partitions and doors could fall under any of the headings of qualifying plant set out above: but tax is like that sometimes!

In Summary

Whilst buildings themselves are rarely eligible for capital allowances, we can now see that a great deal of expenditure on property, and within property, will qualify for capital allowances. In fact, there is an entire industry of specialists able to identify and maximise claims for capital allowances on property.

But beware, the availability of these allowances is now under serious threat and we will return to look at the future of capital allowances claims on fixtures within property in Chapter 8.

2.5   INTEGRAL FEATURES

In April 2008, a whole new category of plant and machinery within property was created: 'integral features'.

The new category combined some items which would previously have appeared on our list in Section 2.4, and would have qualified as plant and machinery in their own right, and some items which previously would not have qualified for capital allowances at all.

The items classed as integral features are:

- Electrical lighting and power systems
- Cold water systems
- Space or water heating systems, air conditioning, ventilation and air purification systems and floors or ceilings comprised in such systems
- Lifts, escalators and moving walkways
- External solar shading

In short, integral features include all the wiring, lighting, plumbing, heating and air conditioning in any qualifying property purchased since April 2008 and all these items qualify as plant and machinery for capital allowances purposes.

Combined with the other items which we looked at in Section 2.4, this means that a considerable proportion of the cost of many properties qualifies for capital allowances: which is why the changes we will be looking at in Chapter 8 are so important!

The creation of the integral features category has considerably enhanced the availability of capital allowances on business property. The downside, however, is that, unless the expenditure is covered by the annual investment allowance, it will fall into the special rate pool and attract writing down allowances at just 10% (falling to just 8% from April 2012).

2.6 REPAIRS TO INTEGRAL FEATURES

Where any business spends money on repairs to an 'integral feature', on which it is entitled to claim capital allowances, and that expenditure, over any period of twelve months (not necessarily the business's accounting period) amounts to more than half of the cost of replacing the entire feature, the relevant expenditure has to be classed as capital expenditure for tax purposes. The expenditure is then classed as plant and machinery and capital allowances may be claimed in the usual way.

Example

Crollaberry Ltd draws up accounts to 31st December each year. The company owns its own business premises which have a troublesome old central heating system. It would cost £20,000 to replace the entire system.

In October 2011, the company had some repairs done to the heating system at a cost of £2,500. However, this was not enough and, in January 2012, the boiler had to be replaced at a cost of £6,500. The engineer who carried out the work also advised the company that it needed to replace some of the radiators and that this would cost a further £2,000.

If Crollaberry Ltd has the radiators replaced before the anniversary of the first set of expenditure in October 2011, it will have spent £11,000: more than half of the cost of replacing the entire central heating system. All of this expenditure would then need to be treated as capital expenditure, the company would be unable to claim it as a repair cost, and would need to claim capital allowances instead.

Whether any of this matters to Crollaberry Ltd will depend on whether it has fully utilised its annual investment allowance in the years ending 31st December 2011 and 2012.

If there is enough annual investment allowance still available to cover the expenditure in both years, it will not make any difference to the company's overall tax position if the repairs have to be treated as capital expenditure.

On the other hand, however, if there is insufficient annual investment allowance remaining in either year, the company might be well advised to defer replacing the radiators until after twelve months have elapsed since the repair work in October 2011. It will then be able to claim all £11,000 of expenditure as repair costs.

2.7   PURCHASES, REPLACEMENTS AND NEW INSTALLATIONS

The assets listed in Sections 2.4 and 2.5 currently qualify for capital allowances in much the same way regardless of whether they are purchased as part of a second-hand, property, or are newly installed in the property by the current owner.

However, there are some restrictions on the value which may be assigned to qualifying assets within a second-hand property and we will look at these in detail in Chapter 8, together with the Government's proposals for additional restrictions and time limits to apply from April 2012 onwards.

Replacement assets may also qualify for capital allowances, although some of these will be classed as repairs: particularly replacement fixtures not caught by the special rules set out in Section 2.6.

For a detailed examination of the tax treatment of replacement assets within property, see the Taxcafe.co.uk guide *'How to Avoid Property Tax'*.

2.8 CAPITAL ALLOWANCES FOR LANDLORDS

Many people are under the mistaken impression that landlords are not entitled to capital allowances.

This is simply not the case. As we saw in Section 1.2, all types of property rental are qualifying activities for capital allowances purposes.

However, there are two key exclusions applying to landlords which we need to be aware of:

i) Firstly, landlords cannot claim capital allowances on any assets used within a rented 'dwelling house'. We will take a more detailed look at what this means in Section 2.10.

ii) Secondly, landlords cannot generally claim first year allowances on assets within their rented properties.

There are some important exceptions to the second exclusion. The enhanced capital allowances on energy-saving plant and machinery and environmentally beneficial plant and machinery (see Section 1.5) remain available to landlords in the case of 'background' plant and machinery.

Broadly speaking, 'background' plant and machinery generally means any assets which qualify for capital allowances and which are 'affixed to, or otherwise installed in' a rented property. This is therefore likely to cover all integral features (see Section 2.5) and many of the other items listed in Section 2.4, but will generally **not** cover:

- Manufacturing and processing equipment
- Storage and display equipment and checkouts
- Furniture (although fixed seating is covered)
- Hoists
- Decorative assets provided for the enjoyment of the public (in hotels, restaurants, and other similar establishments)

Although it would be rare that any such items qualified for the enhanced capital allowances described in Section 1.5 in any case!

Sadly, it does not look as if landlords will be entitled to the new first year allowance on plant and machinery within properties located in assisted areas within enterprise zones (see Section 1.5).

The good news, however, is that the exclusion relating to first year allowances does not apply to the annual investment allowance. Apart from the other exclusion for assets within rented dwelling-houses, landlords remain fully eligible for the annual investment allowance on assets within rented property.

It is also important to remember that neither of the exclusions described above have any effect on landlords' ability to claim capital allowances on other assets used in their business, but which are not located within their rental properties, such as: their own computer, other office equipment and furniture, their car, and any qualifying assets within their own business premises.

2.9 COMMERCIAL PROPERTY

Apart from the possible restrictions on first year allowances described in Section 2.8, landlords generally remain eligible to claim capital allowances on fixtures and fittings which they have installed, or otherwise purchased, within their rented commercial property.

There are, however, a few risk areas which need to be considered.

Firstly, landlords may lose the right to capital allowances on fixtures and fittings within a commercial property if they grant a long lease (two years or more) to a tenant and charge a lease premium. As such a premium is wholly or partly regarded as a capital sum for tax purposes, the landlord will be treated as having made a partial disposal of the property and may therefore lose the right to claim any capital allowances on assets within it.

A landlord may also lose the right to claim capital allowances on any items not qualifying as 'background' plant and machinery (see Section 2.8) when a property is leased for more than five years. However, this should not generally apply to assets on which the landlord had been able to claim capital allowances previously, before the commencement of the new lease.

Finally, landlords may also lose the right to capital allowances on any fixtures or fittings which they lease to the tenant separately under a different agreement to the lease of the property itself. However, this particular problem can often be avoided by making a joint election with the tenant. Furthermore, this can also be a useful method to enable the landlord to retain the right to capital allowances on assets within the property where a long lease has been granted at a premium as described above.

2.10 RESIDENTIAL PROPERTY

As explained in Section 2.8, landlords are not entitled to claim capital allowances on any assets used within a rented 'dwelling house'.

Many people view this as a complete ban on capital allowances on any assets within residential property but this is not the case. It is true that most residential property landlords cannot claim capital allowances on assets within their rental properties but capital allowances do remain available on all qualifying assets (as listed in Sections 2.3 to 2.5) within:

- Qualifying furnished holiday lettings (see Section 2.11)
- Residential property used in a trade (e.g. as accommodation for employees, or for visiting customers or suppliers)
- Communal areas not falling within any rented 'dwelling house'

Communal areas typically arise in the case of properties which have been divided into self-contained flats. The areas within the property lying outside the flats are not within any 'dwelling house' and assets within those areas can therefore qualify for capital allowances.

This gives some residential landlords the opportunity to make significant capital allowances claims on assets within communal areas, especially in the case of properties purchased since April 2008: as claims for a proportion of the 'integral features' (see Section 2.5) in the property will be available.

Properties divided into self-contained flats have always qualified for some capital allowances but recent changes made by HM Revenue and Customs mean that many other landlords renting out HMOs (houses in multiple occupation) may also be able to make significant capital allowances claims. We will take a detailed look at this issue in Chapter 9.

2.11 FURNISHED HOLIDAY LETTINGS

Assets, including integral features, within qualifying furnished holiday lettings are eligible for capital allowances.

The current qualification requirements for a property to be regarded as a furnished holiday letting are set out below. The increased requirements applying from the 2012/13 tax year (the year ending 5th April 2013) onwards are included in brackets.

i)   The property must be situated in the European Economic Area (see Appendix B)
ii) The property must be furnished (to at least the minimum level which an occupier would usually expect)
iii) It must be let out on a commercial basis with a view to the realisation of profits
iv) It must be available for commercial letting to the public generally for at least 140 days in a 12-month period (210 days from 2012/13)
v)   It must be so let for at least 70 such days (105 days from 2012/13)
vi) The property must not normally be in the same occupation for more than 31 consecutive days at any time during a period of at least seven months out of the same 12-month period as that referred to in (iv) above

The 12-month period referred to in (iv) and (vi) above is normally the tax year ending on 5th April.

From the tax year 2010/11 onwards, landlords can elect for properties which qualified for the furnished holiday letting regime under the above criteria in the previous year to stay within the regime for up to two further tax years despite failing to meet the test under (v) above. In effect, this means that properties will generally only need to meet this test once every three years. The property will still need to meet all of the other tests, however, and the landlord must make genuine efforts to meet the test under (v) every year.

A taxpayer with more than one furnished holiday letting property may also use a system of averaging to determine whether they meet test (v). This extension cannot, however, be used in conjunction with the two year extension described above: properties must qualify in their own right before the two year extension can be claimed.

Other Qualification Issues

Whilst the property need not be in a recognised holiday area, the lettings should strictly be to holidaymakers and tourists in order to qualify.

Where a property qualifies, as set out above, then it generally qualifies for the whole of each qualifying tax year, subject to special rules for the years in which holiday letting commences or ceases.

2.12 LOSS RELIEF FOR LANDLORDS

An additional benefit provided to individual landlords by capital allowances is the fact that any allowances in excess of the landlord's rental profits may be set off against the landlord's other income for the same tax year or the next.

Individual landlords making rental losses can set all their capital allowances against other income, such as employment, trading or investment income, often leading to some very useful tax repayments.

This is highly beneficial to individual landlords since the remainder of their rental losses can only be carried forward to be set off against future rental profits.

Companies have greater scope to relieve rental losses in any case, so the additional facility for setting off capital allowances does not provide any further benefit.

Wealth Warning

The Government is considering introducing restrictions on the ability to set capital allowances against an individual landlord's other income after 5th April 2013.

Landlords who may be entitled to significant capital allowances may therefore wish to consider bringing the relevant projects forward to 2011/12 or 2012/13 in order to be able to offset their allowances against other taxable income.

Furnished Holiday Lettings

Sadly, the facility to set capital allowances in excess of rental profits off against other income is no longer available for capital allowances on assets used in a furnished holiday letting business.

2.13 LANDLORDS AND CAPITAL ALLOWANCES: SUMMARY

To summarise the position, landlords may claim capital allowances on qualifying assets within:

- Rented commercial property
- Furnished holiday lettings
- Communal areas within residential property
- Their own business premises

But **not** on assets within:

- Rented dwelling houses

They may also claim capital allowances on their own equipment, such as computers, office furniture and equipment, cars and vans.

The only further disadvantage which landlords suffer is that they cannot generally claim first year allowances (with some important exceptions). But, they can claim the annual investment allowance.

Hence, despite the restrictions discussed in this chapter, landlords
are eligible to claim far more capital allowances than many people
realise.

However, the considerable benefits currently available are set to be
significantly eroded by changes coming up in the near future.
Many landlords could therefore benefit by accelerating future
expenditure into an earlier period (subject to the transitional rules
in Chapter 7), or by making capital allowances claims on past
expenditure now (see Sections 4.3 and 4.4).

Chapter 3

Other Important Allowances

3.1 THE BUSINESS PREMISES RENOVATION ALLOWANCE

The 'Business Premises Renovation Allowance' provides a 100% first year allowance for costs incurred in renovating or converting disused commercial property in designated 'assisted areas' to bring it back into business use. These areas can be found in the Assisted Areas Order SI 2007/107, which is available online.

The new 'business use' need not be the same as the building's original use and can include offices and shops. Some businesses are excluded, however, including fisheries, shipbuilding, coal, steel, synthetic fibres and a number of agricultural activities.

The relief is available to both owner-occupiers and landlords letting the property out to qualifying businesses following renovation.

The property must have been vacant for at least a year prior to the commencement of renovation work. Where part of a property has been vacant for a year or more, relief may be claimed for the cost of work on that part of the property.

The relief is confined to the cost of renovation or conversion. Purchase costs and the costs of building any extensions (except where built merely to provide access) are excluded from relief. Any costs covered by a grant are also excluded.

The claimant may choose not to claim the first year allowance in full and may, instead, claim the lower of the unrelieved balance or 25% of the qualifying expenditure in each year until the claim is exhausted.

This relief was originally introduced for a fixed period which was due to expire on 11th April 2012, but it has now been extended for a further five years, to April 2017.

3.2   FLAT CONVERSION ALLOWANCES

In an effort to regenerate some of the UK's urban centres, a special tax incentive known as 'Flat Conversion Allowances' was introduced in 2001. Sadly, however, this potentially valuable relief is to be withdrawn for expenditure incurred after 31st March 2013 by companies, or after 5th April 2013 by other business entities.

Anyone interested in the renovation or conversion of old residential property should therefore act quickly to secure this relief while it is still available.

Broadly speaking, what this allowance does is to enable you to make an immediate claim against your taxable income for the costs of converting qualifying properties back into residential flats.

Furthermore, as long as you keep these flats for a sufficient length of time after completing the conversion work, the allowance will never be clawed back, meaning that Cameron, Clegg & Co. will, for once, have actually made a contribution in return for their silent partnership stake in your business!

To qualify for the allowance, the flats must be in a property which was built before 1980 and has no more than five floors in total. The ground floor must be in business use, such as a shop, café, office or doctor's surgery, and the upper storeys must originally have been constructed primarily for residential occupation.

Additionally, in the year before conversion takes place, the storeys above the ground floor must have been used only for storage purposes or been unoccupied.

In other words, the allowance is given for converting vacant property back into residential property.

Example

Priyanka is a higher rate taxpayer with total annual taxable income of well over £100,000. In June 2012, she buys a run-down three storey property on Kirkcaldy High Street.

Despite having once been the site where Adam Smith wrote his 'Wealth of Nations', the ground floor is now leased to a rather poor quality fast-food retailer.

However, Priyanka is more interested in the upper storeys which are currently unoccupied and in a state of disrepair. She spends £60,000 converting these storeys into a number of small flats which she then lets out.

Not only does Priyanka now have a valuable property and a stream of rental income, but she will also be able to cut her tax bill this year by up to £30,000!

As long as she continues to own the flats for a further seven years after the conversion, this money will never be clawed back.

The only drawback (there has to be one, doesn't there?) is that Priyanka cannot claim this same expenditure in her Capital Gains Tax computation when she eventually sells the flats. There is still a major benefit for Priyanka, however, since she is getting the certainty of 'up front' tax relief now at between 40% and 50%.

There are some restrictions on the type of flat which you can create out of the conversion. Basically, they have to be small and not particularly luxurious.

The type of expenditure which can be claimed is also restricted and excludes, in particular, the original cost of the property prior to conversion, the cost of any extensions to the property and the cost of furnishing the flats.

Still, on the whole, this is a pretty useful allowance but time is fast running out for anyone wishing to make the most of it!

Chapter 4

Capital Allowances Planning

4.1 PLANNING FOR CHANGE

Before we move on to take a detailed look at the changes ahead, we need to take a look at some important tax planning techniques which are currently available under the capital allowances regime as it stands today.

Some of the issues which we will look at in this chapter are essential to understanding both the importance of the changes which lie ahead and also some of the methods which businesses will be able to utilise to minimise the adverse impact of those changes.

We will also pick up a few additional points of interest in this chapter.

4.2 SHORT-LIFE ASSETS

Short-life asset elections are a useful tax planning tool which enable businesses to obtain full relief for the economic cost of an asset over its working life rather than wait for many years to obtain it through writing down allowances alone.

A short-life asset election means that an asset is effectively 'depooled' and kept in its own separate pool for capital allowances purposes until the expiry of a statutory 'cut-off period'. If the asset is sold or scrapped during this period, a balancing allowance or charge arises; if not, the remaining balance is transferred to the general pool.

Cars, integral features and other assets falling into the special rate pool are ineligible. Assets with partial private use owned by sole traders or partnerships are automatically depooled in any case, so no election would be necessary.

For assets purchased after 5th April 2011 (31st March 2011 for companies), the 'cut-off period' is eight years from the end of the accounting period in which the asset was purchased. This is double the 'cut-off period' of four years applying to earlier purchases.

The time limit for making a short life asset election is two years from the end of the accounting period for Corporation Tax purposes or one year after the 31st January following the relevant tax year for Income Tax purposes.

Combining the increased cut-off period with the other changes to capital allowances applying from April 2012, it will become far more important to identify suitable assets and make the appropriate elections in future.

Example

During the year ended 31st December 2011, Lightyear Limited spent £150,000 on new machinery, including a wing-making machine bought for £50,000 in May 2011.

The wing-making machine is eventually scrapped in December 2019 and the company receives just £300 for it.

If the company had made a short-life asset election in respect of the machine (by 31st December 2013) it would get a balancing allowance of £9,611 in 2019. Otherwise, in the absence of such an election, the same balance would simply remain in the general pool attracting a writing down allowance of just 18% (see Section 5.2).

4.3 LATE CLAIMS

At present, it is possible to claim capital allowances on qualifying expenditure incurred at almost any point in the past provided that:

i) The relevant asset is still owned by the claimant and being used in the business on the first day of the period for which the claim is made, and
ii) The expenditure qualified for capital allowances at the time that it was incurred.

Hence, a business could claim capital allowances on any previously unclaimed qualifying expenditure provided that it still owns the relevant asset. The claim must be based on the cost of the relevant asset at the time of purchase and it will not be possible to claim for items which did not qualify at that time. In this context, it is important to remember that cold water systems, electrical systems and lighting did not generally qualify before April 2008.

Both first year allowances and the annual investment allowance are only available for expenditure incurred in the year for which the claim is made, however, so most past expenditure will only attract writing down allowances. Nevertheless, where large sums are involved, a claim will still be well worthwhile.

This facility to claim allowances on past expenditure is now under threat in the case of integral features and other fixtures within property. We will look at the consequences of this in detail in Chapter 8 but, for the moment, it is worth just saying that businesses owning any commercial property, furnished holiday lettings, or residential property with communal areas, would be well advised to carry out a review of their property to see if there are any items of qualifying plant and machinery on which they have not yet claimed capital allowances.

4.4   NOT-SO-LATE CLAIMS

In the context of late capital allowances claims, it is worth noting that, for Income Tax purposes, it is possible to amend a Tax Return at any time up until the 31st January after the anniversary of the end of the relevant tax year.

Hence, in most cases, capital allowances claims by sole traders or partnerships for accounting periods ending between 6th April 2009 and 5th April 2010 can still be made up until 31st January 2012. Likewise, claims for periods ending between 6th April 2010 and 5th April 2011 can still be made up until 31st January 2013.

Combining this with the ability to make claims for past expenditure (discussed in Section 4.3) means that any business owner who discovers that they have failed to claim capital allowances on qualifying plant and machinery in the past can quickly catch up on a lot of their missing tax relief.

Example

Yvonne is a sole trader drawing up accounts to 30th June each year.

In January 2012 she realises that she has failed to claim capital allowances on £10,000 worth of qualifying plant and machinery in each of the ten years up to and including the year ended 30th June 2010. All of the qualifying assets are still in use in her business and would fall into the general pool if claimed.

Acting quickly, Yvonne is able to amend her 2010 Tax Return before 31st January 2012. She claims additional capital allowances for the year ended 30th June 2009 as follows:

Annual investment allowance:	*£10,000*
(on qualifying expenditure during the year ended 30th June 2009)	
Writing down allowances:	*£16,000*
(at 20% on qualifying expenditure of £10,000 in each of the previous eight years)	

Yvonne is also able to amend her 2011 Tax Return by making the following additional capital allowances claims:

Annual investment allowance:	*£10,000*
(on qualifying expenditure during the year ended 30th June 2010)	
Writing down allowances:	*£12,800*
(at 20% on the unrelieved balance of qualifying expenditure incurred in the years ended 30th June 2001 to 2008)	

Hence, Yvonne has already managed to claw back £48,800 of the missing relief on her previous qualifying expenditure of £100,000 and this will significantly reduce her Income Tax liability due on 31st January 2012. She also has a further balance of £51,200 carried forward in her general pool which will provide additional tax relief in future years.

As we can see from the example, the ability to claim relief on past expenditure can be extremely valuable.

Companies

Companies have until the second anniversary of the date on which their accounting period ended to amend their Corporation Tax Returns, including amendments to capital allowances claims.

4.5 DISCLAIMERS

Apart from balancing allowances and charges, capital allowances are not mandatory. All other capital allowances on plant and machinery may be 'disclaimed'. In fact, any proportion of the available allowance from zero to 100% may be claimed.

Any 'disclaimed' element of the annual investment allowance, or any first year allowances which are available, will fall into the general pool or special rate pool, as appropriate, and will attract writing down allowances at the appropriate rate applying.

Disclaimers of capital allowances are useful in a number of situations where the allowance might otherwise go to waste, such as in the case of a small business whose owner has insufficient income to use their income tax personal allowance.

Rather than claim an allowance which will effectively be wasted, a disclaimer means that greater allowances will be available in future years.

Example

Joe has a business profit for the 2011/12 tax year of just £5,000 before capital allowances. He has no other income. During the year he bought a new machine for £4,000 and could claim an annual investment allowance of £4,000, reducing his taxable profit to just £1,000.

This would be pointless, however, as Joe's profit is less than both his personal allowance and his national insurance earnings threshold and is therefore already tax free anyway. Joe therefore disclaims his annual investment allowance in 2011/12 which means he has no capital allowances claim for the current tax year. His expenditure of £4,000 falls into his general pool and he will be able to claim a writing down allowance of £720 (18%) in the next tax year: 2012/13. This may not be much, but it is better than wasting his allowance altogether.

Later, Joe realises that, whilst he will be paying basic rate Income Tax at 20% for 2012/13, he is likely to make enough profit to push him into the higher rate tax bracket for 2013/14.

He wonders, therefore, if he should disclaim his £720 allowance in 2012/13 in order to benefit from greater tax savings in 2013/14.

Joe speaks to his accountant, Sylvia, about this but her answer is an emphatic "no!" Sylvia explains that by disclaiming his £720 allowance in 2012/13, Joe will pay an extra £144 in Income Tax (at 20%) and £65 in National Insurance (at 9%).

"Yeah", responds Joe, "but surely I'll save much more next year when I'm paying tax at 40%".

"No, you won't", responds Sylvia. "If you claim your £720 allowance in 2012/13, you will still have unrelieved expenditure of £3,280 to carry forward and that will give you an allowance of £590 next year anyway. The disclaimer would therefore only give you an extra allowance of £130 next year, so you'd only save £55, even with a 42% combined rate of Income Tax and National Insurance. It's just not worth it."

"Oh", says Joe. "Well, thanks for putting me straight, I don't know how I'd cope without you pulling the strings."

The lesson here is that a capital allowances disclaimer is generally worthwhile when the allowance would have gone to waste otherwise, but is seldom beneficial in other cases.

One other situation where a disclaimer might be worthwhile, however, is where a business is entitled to the temporary first year allowance (at 40%) for expenditure incurred during the 2009/10 tax year (or between 1st April 2009 and 31st March 2010 for a company), but would face a balancing charge if it claimed it. This situation could only arise, however, if the business has:

i) Disposal proceeds on the sale of qualifying plant and machinery in excess of the balance of unrelieved expenditure brought forward on the relevant pool (either the general pool or the special rate pool), and
ii) Purchases of new qualifying plant and machinery in excess of its maximum annual investment allowance for the period.

Example

At 1st January 2010, Henson Limited had unrelieved expenditure brought forward on its general pool of £10,000.

In March 2010, the company sold its old 'Golden Boots' digging machine, for £40,000 and replaced it with a new 'Silver Boots' digger, at a cost of £100,000. As the new machine was purchased before 1st April 2010, the maximum annual investment allowance available is just £50,000, but the company is entitled to claim first year allowances at 40% on the balance (see Section 1.5).

However, if the company claims the first year allowance available on the Silver Boots digger in full, the capital allowances computation for the year ended 31st December 2010 will look like this:

	£	£
Tax written down value Brought forward		10,000
Less: Sale proceeds of machine sold	40,000	

Shortfall in pool value – Balancing charge:		30,000
		=====
New purchases	100,000	
Less: Annual Investment Allowance	50,000	

	50,000	
Less: First Year Allowance at 40%	20,000	

Tax written down value Carried forward		30,000
		=====

Total net amount of capital allowances claimed: £50,000 + £20,000 LESS the balancing charge of £30,000 = £40,000.

As we can see, the sale of Henson Limited's old digging machine has caused a balancing charge to arise, even despite the 'pooling' of all the company's plant and equipment for capital allowances purposes. However, it is possible to refrain from claiming the first year allowance in full.

When first year allowances are not claimed on a new purchase (known as a 'disclaimer'), the relevant expenditure is immediately added to the tax written down value of the pool before any balancing charge can be calculated.

Hence, although a first year allowance of 40% is being sacrificed, the same expenditure is effectively being relieved at 100% by preventing a balancing charge from arising.

Furthermore, it is possible to achieve an optimum result by disclaiming only the exact amount necessary to prevent a balancing charge. It is not necessary to match the amount disclaimed to a specific machine, asset or group of assets. Let's return to the example to see this in action.

Example Continued

Taking advice from their accountants, Henson Limited's directors decide to disclaim first year allowances on £30,000 of their new purchase expenditure. The company's capital allowances computation for the year ending 31st December 2010 now looks like this:

	£	£
Tax written down value		
Brought forward	10,000	
Add:		
New expenditure on which first		
year allowances not claimed	30,000	

	40,000	
Less:		
Sale proceeds of machine sold	40,000	

Net pool balance remaining		0
		=====
New purchases	100,000	
Less:		
Amount disclaimed	30,000	

	70,000	
Less: Annual Investment Allowance	50,000	

	20,000	
Less:		
First Year Allowance at 40%	8,000	

Tax written down value		
Carried forward		12,000
		=====

*Total net amount of capital allowances claimed: £50,000 + £8,000 = £58,000, i.e. **£18,000 more** than before the disclaimer!*

4.6 WHY BALANCING CHARGES ARE BECOMING MORE COMMON

Prior to 2008, balancing charges did not generally arise on disposals of plant and machinery used wholly in the business. This is because any sale proceeds received were simply deducted from the balance on the general pool. Hence, no balancing charge could arise on these assets unless the business ceased or one or more of the assets were sold for a sum in excess of the balance on the pool.

So, what's changed?

Well, the principle that any sale proceeds are deducted from the unrelieved balance of expenditure in the pool remains true, albeit slightly complicated by the fact that we now have the special rate pool to consider as well as the general pool.

What has changed, however, is the fact that, due to the annual investment allowance, most small businesses now have little or no balance of unrelieved expenditure left. Hence, there will often be a balancing charge whenever any asset used in the business is sold.

Chapter 5

Changes Ahead!

5.1 OVERVIEW

We have already seen a number of changes to the capital allowances regime which have taken place recently, or which are due to take place over the next couple of years, earlier in this guide. In the next few chapters, however, we are going to look at the major changes about to take place on 1st April 2012 for companies and on 6th April 2012 for other businesses.

The changes come in two fundamental areas:

- Reductions in the rates of capital allowances available on all plant and machinery
- Restrictions on capital allowances claims on fixtures in second-hand property

In the next three chapters we will be looking at the impact of the reductions in capital allowances rates. We will then look at the restrictions on fixtures in second-hand property in Chapter 8.

For the rest of this guide, I will be referring to various capital allowances terminology used under the existing regime. All of the various terms were explained in detail in Chapters 1 and 2.

5.2 REDUCTIONS IN CAPITAL ALLOWANCES RATES

From 1st April 2012 for companies, and 6th April 2012 for other businesses, capital allowances rates will be reduced as follows:

- The maximum annual investment allowance available for an accounting period of 12 months will be reduced from £100,000 to just £25,000.
- The rate of writing down allowances on the general pool will be reduced from 20% to 18%.
- The rate of writing down allowances on the special rate pool will be reduced from 10% to 8%.

Transitional rules apply to all accounting periods which span the date of change on 1st or 6th April 2012. We will examine these in detail in Chapter 7.

5.3 REDUCTIONS IN RATES ON CARS

From April 2012, the reduced writing down allowances rate of 18% will also apply to cars with CO_2 emissions of more than 110g/km but no more than 160g/km and the reduced rate of 8% will apply to cars with CO_2 emissions of over 160g/km.

Furthermore, from 1st April 2013, all cars with CO_2 emissions of no more than 160g/km will only attract writing down allowances at just 18%, as the 100% first year allowance currently applying to cars with CO_2 emissions of 110g/km or less will no longer be available.

Company cars will continue to be added to the general pool or special rate pool as appropriate and it will therefore take many years to obtain tax relief for their true economic cost.

For example, where a company car with CO_2 emissions of over 110g/km but no more than 160g/km is purchased for £20,000 during an accounting period ending 31st March 2013 and then sold for £5,000 four years later, its true economic cost is £15,000, but it will take until the year ending 31st March 2024 to even obtain relief for £14,000 out of this sum.

Worse still, if the same car had CO_2 emissions in excess of 160g/km, it would take until the year ending 31st March 2043 to obtain £14,000 worth of relief – that's 30 years since the car was bought, 26 years since it was sold, and £1,000 of its cost is still not subject to any tax relief!

Business owners' own cars will continue to be placed in separate pools so, whilst the reduction in writing down allowances will reduce the tax relief available during the owner's ownership of the car, the full cost (less sale proceeds) will continue to be relieved by the time the car is sold.

5.4 THE IMPACT OF THE REDUCTIONS

Most businesses will feel the impact of the capital allowances reductions to some degree but it is the size of the business's annual capital expenditure budget which will determine just how badly they are hit.

A small business spending no more than £25,000 per year on qualifying plant and machinery should not be troubled by the reduction in the annual investment allowance – provided that they take care not to fall foul of the transitional rules for periods spanning 1st or 6th April 2012 (see Chapter 7). The biggest problem for these businesses is likely to be the reduction in the writing down allowance rates on cars (see Section 5.3).

Very large businesses spending millions of pounds on plant and machinery each year will not see much difference as a result of the reduction in the annual investment allowance but will be greatly troubled by the reductions in writing down allowance rates.

For expenditure in excess of the annual investment allowance incurred in accounting periods commencing on or after the date of change in April 2012, it will generally take:

- *12 years* to obtain relief for 90% of the cost of most qualifying plant and machinery, or
- *28 years* to obtain relief for 90% of the cost of integral features and other assets falling into the special rate pool

But it is perhaps medium-sized businesses who do not spend millions of pounds on plant and machinery each year, but who do spend in excess of £25,000, who will be hardest hit by the changes in April 2012, as they will suffer both a massive reduction in the amount of expenditure which obtains an immediate 100% deduction under the annual investment allowance and a much lower rate of writing down allowances on the remainder.

Hardest hit of all will be those investing large sums in commercial property or furnished holiday lettings.

For example, a company buying a commercial property during an accounting period ending 31st March 2012 will be able to claim immediate 100% tax relief on up to £100,000 of eligible 'integral features', such as heating, air conditioning, electrical and lighting systems, plumbing, lifts and escalators.

The same company spending £100,000 on the same features after 31st March 2012 would get immediate relief on just £25,000 and a writing down allowance of only 8% on the balance. The same expenditure would thus attract a mere £31,000 in relief in the first year instead of £100,000.

5.5 BEFORE AND AFTER

To further illustrate the impact of the capital allowances reductions for a typical medium-sized trading business, let's look at an example.

Example Part 1 (Before)

Woody is a sole trader running a toy manufacturing business and draws up accounts to 30th April each year. In April 2011, he bought a new workshop and spent a total of £60,000 on integral features within the property. He also bought new equipment for the business at a total cost of £50,000.

Woody is allowed to claim his annual investment allowance on his integral features first. He does this because they would otherwise only get writing down allowances at 10%. This leaves a further £40,000 of the maximum annual investment allowance of £100,000 available for Woody to claim on his new equipment. The last £10,000 of Woody's expenditure attracts writing down allowances at 20%, i.e. £2,000.

Hence, in total, Woody is able to claim capital allowances of £102,000 for the year ended 30th April 2011. The remaining £8,000 of his qualifying expenditure is carried forward in his 'general pool' and will continue to attract writing down allowances in future years.

Example Part 2 (After)

In April 2013, Woody buys another new workshop which again includes a total of £60,000 worth of integral features and he also spends another £50,000 on new equipment.

This time, he can only claim an annual investment allowance of £25,000 on his integral features, leaving £35,000 to fall into the special rate pool where it attracts writing down allowances of just 8%, or £2,800.

As his annual investment allowance has now been exhausted, all of Woody's expenditure on new equipment falls into the general pool and attracts writing down allowances of just 18%, or £9,000.

This time, Woody's capital allowances total just £36,800 (£25,000 + £2,800 + £9,000), compared with £102,000 for exactly the same expenditure two years earlier!

This reduction in his capital allowances could cost Woody up to an extra £33,904 in additional Income Tax (at 50%) and National Insurance (at 2%). That's over half the cost of the integral features in another workshop: not exactly encouraging investment are we Mr Osborne?

As if this weren't bad enough, thanks to the transitional rules for periods spanning the date of change in April 2012, Woody could fare even worse if he invested in another workshop during his current accounting period ending on 30th April 2012. We will look at that potential disaster scenario in Section 7.4.

Chapter 6

Planning for the New Regime

6.1 PLANNING AHEAD

All businesses need to consider how best to optimise their position under the new capital allowances regime and secure as much tax relief for their capital expenditure as possible.

In this chapter, we will look at some of the methods which may be worth considering.

6.2 TIMING YOUR EXPENDITURE

Careful timing of your qualifying plant and machinery expenditure will maximise the amount which is covered by the annual investment allowance and thus qualifies for immediate 100% relief. This has been the case since 2008, when the annual investment allowance was introduced, but will become even more important after April 2012 when the allowance is reduced to just £25,000.

There are, effectively, three aspects to timing to be considered:

i) Maximising the annual investment allowance claim for your last accounting period which ends before 6th April 2012 (or before 1st April 2012 for companies), when most businesses will be entitled to claim up to £100,000.

ii) Spreading expenditure in future years so that the maximum of £25,000 per year can be best utilised.

iii) Avoiding any loss of allowances due to the transitional rules applying to any accounting period which straddles the date of change in April 2012.

We will look at the transitional rules under point (iii) above in Chapter 7. For businesses which never spend more than £25,000 on qualifying plant and machinery (excluding cars) in any year, this is the only aspect which they will usually need to consider.

We will look at the benefits of point (ii) above in the next section. The benefits of point (i) can be illustrated by way of an example.

Example

Lexington Ltd usually spends £40,000 each year on new qualifying plant and machinery. The company has a 31st March accounting date. If it sticks to its usual expenditure pattern, it will be eligible for the following capital allowances:

Year ending 31st March 2012:
Annual investment allowance   £40,000

Year ending 31st March 2013:
Annual investment allowance   £25,000
Writing down allowances   £2,700

Year ending 31st March 2014:
Annual investment allowance   £25,000
Writing down allowances   £4,914

Three year total: £97,614

Instead, however, the company brings forward an additional £30,000 of planned expenditure into the year ending 31st March 2012 so that the total qualifying expenditure for that year is £70,000. It then spends £25,000 in each of the next two years so that its total expenditure over the three years remains £120,000, as originally budgeted. The company will now be eligible for the following capital allowances:

Year ending 31st March 2012:
Annual investment allowance   £70,000

Year ending 31st March 2013:
Annual investment allowance   £25,000

Year ending 31st March 2014:
Annual investment allowance   £25,000

Three year total: £120,000

By carefully planning the timing of its expenditure, the company has gained an extra £22,386 in capital allowances over the three year period.

Note that, in this example, I have assumed that all of the company's qualifying expenditure falls into the general pool. I have also ignored any balance brought forward on the pool at 1st April 2011.

The downside to this form of planning is that additional purchases have to be financed earlier than originally planned. The commercial implications of this must naturally be taken into account.

However, it is worth bearing in mind that Lexington Limited will save somewhere between £4,477 and £6,313 in Corporation Tax over the three years as a result of this planning: which will certainly help to finance those earlier purchases!

Tax Tip

Lexington Limited's maximum saving is enhanced by the fact that the main rate of Corporation Tax is being reduced over the next few years.

Hence, for any company with profits in excess of £300,000, accelerating their qualifying expenditure will not only accelerate their capital allowances claims, but will also mean that relief is obtained at a higher rate.

6.3 SPREADING EXPENDITURE

In Section 6.2, we looked at the benefits of accelerating qualifying expenditure on plant and machinery in order to accelerate capital allowances claims.

Accelerating expenditure will almost always be beneficial for tax purposes when the accelerated expenditure is covered by the annual investment allowance.

In some cases, however, it may be more beneficial to defer some qualifying expenditure.

This will occur where a business does not have a regular expenditure pattern and, in years commencing after 31st March 2012, spends, or otherwise might spend, more than £25,000 in a year.

Example

Cody is a sole trader with a 30th September accounting date. He does not usually spend any significant amounts on qualifying plant and machinery.

In August 2013, however, Cody purchases new business premises. He enters into a joint election with the seller to fix the value of the qualifying plant and machinery within the property at £30,000. All of this qualifying expenditure relates to integral features and therefore falls into the special rate pool.

Cody is advised that further expenditure of £20,000 is required to fit out the property and that this will all qualify for capital allowances but will also fall into the special rate pool.

If Cody goes ahead and has the additional work on the property done before 30th September 2013, he will have total qualifying expenditure for the year of £50,000. He would then be able to claim a £25,000 annual investment allowance plus writing down allowances of £2,000 (at 8%) on the remainder. He would also be able to claim writing down allowances of £1,840 in the following year, giving him total allowances of £28,840 over the two year period.

Alternatively, however, if Cody waits until October (i.e. after his year end) to have the additional work done, he would only have spent £30,000 during the year ending 30th September 2013. His capital allowances claim for the year would then amount to £25,400: an annual investment allowance of £25,000 and writing down allowances of £400.

The following year, Cody would be able to claim the annual investment allowance on his £20,000 of fitting out expenditure plus a further £368 in writing down allowances, bringing his total claim over the two year period to £45,768.

Hence, by deferring the additional £20,000 of expenditure, Cody would gain an additional £16,928 in capital allowances over a two year period. As a higher rate taxpayer, this could save him up to £7,110 in Income Tax (at 40%) and National Insurance (at 2%).

See Section 8.9 regarding the importance of the joint election referred to in the above example.

This planning again has commercial implications: not financing accelerated expenditure, but the implications of deferring expenditure which is required for the business. As usual, these need to be weighed against the tax savings arising.

6.4 ALLOCATING THE ANNUAL INVESTMENT ALLOWANCE

I have mentioned it several times already in this guide, but it is worth repeating here that the annual investment allowance can generally be allocated to any qualifying expenditure incurred during the accounting period.

There are a few exceptions, most notably cars, but the most important point is that it can be allocated to integral features and other assets falling into the special rate pool in preference to assets falling into the general pool.

This is an important piece of planning because allocating the annual investment allowance to integral features and other items in the special rate pool will increase your capital allowances claims by 92% of the qualifying expenditure after April 2012 (100% - 8%).

Allocating the annual investment allowance to assets in the general pool will only increase your capital allowances claim by 82% of the qualifying expenditure (100% - 18%).

Furthermore, as we saw in Section 5.4, it takes a lot longer to obtain relief on assets in the special rate pool which are not covered by the annual investment allowance.

6.5 USING OTHER ALLOWANCES

As well as allocating the annual investment allowance to assets falling into the special rate pool, there are a number of other assets which you should ***not*** allocate it to: namely anything which qualifies for:

- First year allowances at 100% under any of the enhanced capital allowances covered in Section 1.5
- The Business Premises Renovation Allowance (see Section 3.1)
- Flat Conversion Allowances (see Section 3.2)

In the past, many businesses spending less than £100,000 a year on qualifying plant and machinery have seen no reason to spend time identifying potential claims under these provisions. In the future, however, with the annual investment allowance reduced to just £25,000, such time could be well spent!

6.6   USING SHORT-LIFE ASSET ELECTIONS

Another area of planning worth looking into will be short-life asset elections. As we saw in Section 4.2, any qualifying assets which you can identify with a working life of eight years or less, and a low residual value thereafter, can be depooled and will attract a balancing allowance on disposal.

Where a business is spending more than the maximum amount of the annual investment allowance for the relevant period, it will be worth identifying these assets, making the relevant elections, and allocating the annual investment allowance elsewhere.

Remember, however, that cars, integral features and other assets falling into the special rate pool are ineligible for short-life asset elections.

6.7   ALLOCATION EXAMPLE

To illustrate the benefits of the techniques discussed in the previous three sections, let's look at an example.

Example

*Mistergee Limited is planning to spend £100,000 on qualifying plant and machinery during the year ending 31**st March 2013. Of this, £20,000 will be spent on integral features.*

Lina, the company's owner, does not realise that the annual investment allowance can be allocated to integral features in preference to other assets and hence she forecasts the resultant capital allowances claims for the next four years as follows:

	General Pool	*Special Rate Pool*
Year ending 31st March 2013:		
Purchases	£80,000	£20,000
Annual investment allowance	(£25,000)	
	£55,000	£20,000
Writing down allowances (at 18%/8%)	(£9,900)	(£1,600)
	£45,100	£18,400
Year ending 31st March 2014:		
Writing down allowances (at 18%/8%)	(£8,118)	(£1,472)
	£36,982	£16,928
Year ending 31st March 2015:		
Writing down allowances (at 18%/8%)	(£6,657)	(£1,354)
	£30,325	£15,574
Year ending 31st March 2016:		
Writing down allowances (at 18%/8%)	(£5,459)	(£1,246)
	£24,866	£14,328

*As we can see, without the benefit of the techniques described in the previous three sections, a total of £39,194 (£24,866 + £14,328) of qualifying expenditure would still remain unrelieved at 31**st March 2016, meaning that the company has received relief on just £60,806 (£100,000 - £39,194).*

We are now going to change Mistergee Limited's capital allowances calculation one step at a time in order to illustrate the benefits of the techniques described in the previous three sections. First of all, we will allocate the annual investment allowance to the integral features:

Phase I: Allocating the Annual Investment Allowance

Allocating the annual investment allowance to the integral features in preference to the company's other expenditure improves its capital allowances claims as follows:

	General Pool	Special Rate Pool
Year ending 31ˢᵗ March 2013:		
Purchases	£80,000	£20,000
Annual investment allowance	(£5,000)	(£20,000)
	-----------	----------
	£75,000	£0
Writing down allowances (at 18%)	(£13,500)	
	-----------	----------
	£61,500	£0
Year ending 31ˢᵗ March 2014: Writing down allowances (at 18%)	(£11,070)	
	-----------	----------
	£50,430	£0
Year ending 31ˢᵗ March 2015: Writing down allowances (at 18%)	(£9,077)	
	-----------	----------
	£41,353	£0
Year ending 31ˢᵗ March 2016: Writing down allowances (at 18%)	(£7,444)	
	-----------	----------
	£33,909	£0
	======	======

After simply introducing the basic technique of allocating the annual investment allowance to assets falling into the special rate pool, the balance of unrelieved expenditure at 31ˢᵗ March 2016 has been reduced to £33,909, meaning that the company has gained an extra £5,285 (£39,194 - £33,909) in allowances over the four year period.

Phase II: Identifying Other Allowances

On reviewing the company's expenditure for the year ending 31st March 2013, Paul, its accountant, notices that £12,000 of the expenditure is eligible for enhanced capital allowances at 100%. Accordingly, he claims these extra allowances and allocates the annual investment allowance elsewhere, with the following result:

	General Pool	Special Rate Pool
Year ending 31st March 2013:		
Purchases	£80,000	£20,000
First year allowances		(£12,000)
Annual investment allowance	(£17,000)	(£8,000)
	-----------	----------
	£63,000	£0
Writing down allowances (at 18%)	(£11,340)	
	-----------	----------
	£51,660	£0
Year ending 31st March 2014:		
Writing down allowances (at 18%)	(£9,299)	
	-----------	----------
	£42,361	£0
Year ending 31st March 2015:		
Writing down allowances (at 18%)	(£7,625)	
	-----------	----------
	£34,736	£0
Year ending 31st March 2016:		
Writing down allowances (at 18%)	(£6,252)	
	-----------	----------
	£28,484	£0
	======	======

The enhanced capital allowances claims have led to a further £5,425 (£33,909 - £28,484) improvement in the company's tax relief over the four year period.

66

Note that, I have assumed here that the items qualifying for enhanced capital allowances would have fallen into the special rate pool rather than the general pool. A review of the lists set out in Section 1.5 indicates that this is probably more likely, but it is actually completely academic, as the same overall result would have arisen if these had been assets in the general pool.

Phase III: Using Short-Life Asset Elections

Amongst the remaining expenditure falling into the general pool, Paul also manages to identify £20,000 of expenditure on items with a working life of only four years which are likely to be scrapped at the end of that period. He therefore makes appropriate short-life asset elections in respect of these items and allocates the annual investment allowance elsewhere.

Assuming that the assets are scrapped (with no sale proceeds arising) during the year ending 31st March 2016, the company's capital allowances calculations will be as set out below.

For ease of illustration, I will leave out the special rate pool this time (which will be exactly as it was in Phase II above), and will treat all of the short-life assets as if they were a single item. In reality, each short-life asset should have its own separate pool.

	General Pool	Short-Life Assets
Year ending 31ˢᵗ March 2013:		
Purchases	£80,000	
Transfer to short-life asset pools	(£20,000)	£20,000
Annual investment allowance	(£17,000)	
	-----------	----------
	£43,000	£20,000
Writing down allowances		
(at 18%)	(£7,740)	(£3,600)
	-----------	----------
	£35,260	£16,400
Year ending 31ˢᵗ March 2014:		
Writing down allowances		
(at 18%)	(£6,347)	(£2,952)
	-----------	----------
	£28,913	£13,448
Year ending 31ˢᵗ March 2015:		
Writing down allowances		
(at 18%)	(£5,204)	(£2,421)
	-----------	----------
	£23,709	£11,027
Year ending 31ˢᵗ March 2016:		
Writing down allowances		
(at 18%)	(£4,268)	
Balancing allowances		
on disposal		(£11,027)
	-----------	----------
	£19,441	£0
	======	======

Finally, combining all three techniques, Paul has managed to reduce the amount of unrelieved expenditure remaining at 31ˢᵗ March 2016 to just £19,441, meaning that the company has obtained relief on £80,559 (£100,000 - £19,441) over the four year period.

This is £19,753 (£80,559 - £60,806) more than originally projected by Lina, meaning that the company will have saved between £3,951 and £4,984 in Corporation Tax.

For a higher rate taxpayer sole trader, the same techniques would have produced Income Tax and National Insurance savings of up to £8,296 (£19,753 at 42%).

6.8   ALLOCATION CHECKLIST

To make the most of the capital allowances available to you, especially after April 2012, it is worth bearing this checklist in mind:

1. Do you have any expenditure eligible for enhanced capital allowances at 100%, the Business Premises Renovation Allowance or Flat Conversion Allowances? If so, separate out this expenditure and make the appropriate claim.
2. Allocate the annual investment allowance to any remaining expenditure falling into the special rate pool.
3. Identify any assets which are suitable for a short-life assets election. Separate these out and make the appropriate elections.
4. For sole traders and partnerships: separate out any assets on which allowances must be restricted due to an element of private use.
5. Now allocate any remaining annual investment allowance (after Step 2) to your remaining general pool expenditure.
6. Sole traders and partnerships with any remaining annual investment allowance after Step 5 should allocate it to assets with an element of private use, starting with the assets with the greatest proportion of business use and working down from there.
7. If there is still any annual investment allowance remaining, consider either:
    a. Accelerating additional expenditure so that it falls into the same accounting period (if you still have time), or
    b. Revising Step 3 to reduce the value of assets on which you have made short-life assets elections and allocate the remaining annual investment allowance to the items for which you no longer make an election.

This checklist does not cover cars. We will look at planning techniques for cars in Sections 6.10 to 6.12.

6.9 FINANCE LEASES

Where any business needs to acquire assets with a total value in excess of its maximum annual investment allowance for the relevant period, it may be worth considering obtaining some of the 'excess assets' through finance leases.

From a pure tax perspective alone, finance leases generally provide better tax relief than outright purchases once a business's maximum annual investment allowance for the period has been exhausted.

There are, however, many other tax and non-tax issues to be considered. For a more detailed examination of this subject, see the Taxcafe.co.uk guide *'Small Business Tax Saving Tactics'*.

6.10 PLANNING FOR CARS

As we saw in Section 5.3, the reductions in the writing down allowances rates applying from April 2012 will mean that it could take several decades to obtain tax relief on cars in future.

There are a range of potential solutions to this problem, some of which depend on whether we are considering a 'company car', or a business owner's own car (see Section 1.8 for a definition of 'company cars' for this purpose).

In this section, I will look at the potential solutions which are common to both regimes. I will then look at some further potential solutions which are specific to one regime or the other in Sections 6.11 and 6.12.

Solution 1: Lower CO2 Emissions

One solution which is common to both regimes is to buy cars with lower CO_2 emissions. Buying a car with emissions of no more than 160g/km instead of one with emissions above that level increases the rate of writing down allowances from 8% to 18%: a proportionate increase of 125%!

Cars with CO2 emissions of 110g/km or less which are purchased before 1st April 2013 will also attract an immediate tax deduction at 100% (subject to private use adjustments, where applicable).

Solution 2: Vans and Double Cab Pick-ups

Another possibility is to buy a van instead of a car. Vans are eligible for the annual investment allowance and company vans are subject to much lower benefit-in-kind charges for Income Tax purposes than most company cars. VAT-registered businesses can also recover VAT on the cost of the van.

Many 'double cab pick-ups' are classified as vans for tax purposes. These vehicles combine the same comfort and convenience as a typical '4 x 4' with the same tax advantages provided by other vans.

Solution 3: Leasing

From a pure tax perspective alone, many businesses could now be better off holding cars under finance leases rather than purchasing them.

There are some potential exceptions, however, including:

- Non-VAT registered businesses purchasing cars with CO2 emissions of more than 160g/km

- Non-VAT registered businesses purchasing cars with CO2 emissions of no more than 110g/km before 1st April 2013

- Sole traders or business partners buying cars for their own use who expect to have private use of 10% or less, or who expect to be paying a higher rate of tax when they sell the car

For a detailed analysis of the advantages and disadvantages of holding cars under finance leases, see the Taxcafe.co.uk guide *'Small Business Tax Saving Tactics'*.

6.11 BUSINESS OWNERS' CARS

Further solutions available in the case of business owners' own cars (not company directors) include:

Solution 4: Private Use

The simplest solution for business owners' own cars is to make sure that there is some private use of the car. The car must then be put into its own separate pool and will thus attract a balancing allowance on disposal.

Even then, however, the rate of allowances available during the business owner's ownership of the car provides very slow relief and, in many cases, the majority of the relief will only arise when the car is disposed of.

Solution 5: Claim Fixed Mileage Rates

Many sole traders and partnerships may benefit by switching to claiming business mileage at the permitted rates of 45p per mile for the first 10,000 business miles in the tax year (40p per mile before 6th April 2011) and 25p per business mile thereafter.

This method is only available where the business's total annual sales income does not exceed the VAT registration threshold (currently £73,000) and the 'switch' can only be made when a new car is purchased (you cannot change part-way through your ownership of the same car).

Where the fixed mileage rate is being claimed it takes the place of both any capital allowances claims on the vehicle and any claims for actual running costs. In other words, it is claimed instead of these items, not on top of them!

For a full analysis of the potential benefits of switching to claiming fixed mileage rates on a new car used for business purposes, see the Taxcafe.co.uk guide *'Small Business Tax Saving Tactics'*.

6.12 COMPANY CARS

Further solutions available in the case of company cars (including cars provided to company directors by their company) include:

Solution 6: Hold Cars Privately

A director or other employee who uses their own car for business purposes may claim tax-free mileage allowances from their company or employer.

The maximum rates for the tax-free mileage allowances are the same as those which small business owners may claim for business use of their own cars (see Section 6.11).

Whilst tax-free in the director or other employee's hands, the mileage allowances will be eligible for tax relief in the company or employer's own tax computation.

In many cases, this method is more beneficial overall than providing a company car, especially since it also produces Income Tax and National Insurance savings by eliminating the benefit-in-kind charges that arise on company cars.

Chapter 7

The Transitional Rules

7.1 WHO IS AFFECTED?

We've seen how drastically capital allowances will be cut back after April 2012. We now need to consider what happens in the meantime, where a business has an accounting period straddling the date of the changes. Some businesses (like Woody's in Section 5.5) will have started these accounting periods as early as 1st May 2011.

The transitional rules discussed in this chapter affect:

- Companies with accounting periods spanning 1st April 2012, and
- Other businesses with accounting periods spanning 6th April 2012

In other words, the transitional rules affect every business **except**:

- Companies with accounting periods ending on 31st March, and
- Other businesses with accounting periods ending on 5th April

In particular, most individual landlords will be unaffected by the transitional rules, as they are generally required to account for their property income based on accounts for the tax year ended on 5th April.

However, that still leaves a large number of businesses needing to watch out for the huge and unexpected pitfall which we are about to see: a nasty 'sting in the tail' awaits anyone incurring significant qualifying expenditure between the date of the change and their next accounting year end.

7.2 THE ANNUAL INVESTMENT ALLOWANCE

For the most part, the transitional rules operate by a system of simple 'time-apportionment'. In other words, the old rates are applied to the part of the accounting period falling before the date of change and the new rates are applied to the part of the accounting period falling on or after the date of change.

For example, a company with a twelve month accounting period ending on 31st December 2012 will be able to claim a maximum annual investment allowance for the year of:

£100,000 x 91/366 = £24,863
£25,000 x 275/366 = £18,784
Total: £43,647

This maximum annual investment allowance applies to the total expenditure in the accounting period, but an additional rule applies to restrict the amount of expenditure incurred after the date of the change which may qualify.

For expenditure incurred in the part of the accounting period falling on or after the date of change, the maximum annual investment allowance is calculated as if this were a separate accounting period.

Hence, for example, a company with a twelve month accounting period ending on 31st December 2012 can claim an annual investment allowance of up to £43,647, but no more than £18,784 of the qualifying expenditure can take place after 31st March 2012.

In Appendices D and E, I have reproduced the maximum annual investment allowance claims applying to the most common accounting periods straddling the dates of change. The tables in the appendices set out both:

a) The maximum claim for the whole accounting period, and
b) The maximum claim on expenditure incurred on or after the date of change.

It will be readily seen from the appendices that many businesses face a severe restriction on their capital allowances claims for the latter part of any transitional accounting period following the change in capital allowances rates on 1st or 6th April 2012.

The sooner the business's accounting date falls after the date of change, the worse the restriction will be. In Section 7.4, we will see an example of the potential impact.

7.3 WRITING DOWN ALLOWANCES

The rates of writing down allowances applying for periods spanning the date of change are calculated on a simple time apportionment basis and then rounded up to the nearest two decimal places.

For example, the rate of writing down allowances on the general pool for a sole trader with a twelve month accounting period ending 31st October 2012 is:

157/366 x 20% =	8.5792%
209/366 x 18% =	10.2787%
Total:	18.8579%

Which is rounded up to 18.86%.

Similar principles apply to give the same business a rate of 8.86% for the writing down allowances on its special rate pool for the same year.

These transitional rates apply to expenditure incurred at any time in the accounting period, as well as pool balances brought forward from the previous period.

The same rates will also apply to cars. As usual, the general pool rate will apply to cars with CO_2 emissions of more than 110g/km but no more than 160g/km and the rate applying to the special rate pool will also apply to cars with CO_2 emissions of more than 160g/km.

In Appendix F, I have set out the rates of writing down allowances applying to both the general pool and the special rate pool for the most common accounting periods straddling the dates of change.

7.4 THE PRACTICAL IMPACT OF THE TRANSITIONAL RULES

To illustrate the potential impact of the transitional rules in practice, let's return to an earlier example.

For someone like Woody (see Section 5.5), who seems to be in the habit of making most of their capital expenditure towards the end of their accounting period, the transitional rules could prove absolutely disastrous!

Example

Woody is a sole trader and is drawing up accounts for the twelve month accounting period ending 30th April 2012. His maximum annual investment allowance for the whole of this period is:

£100,000 x 341/366 = £93,169
£25,000 x 25/366 =   £1,708
Total   £94,877

Overall, this is not too bad, but what Woody must remember is that the allowance available for expenditure incurred between 6th and 30th April 2012 is just £1,708.

Hence, if Woody spends his usual £60,000 on integral features and £50,000 on other equipment before 6th April 2012, he will be able to claim an annual investment allowance of £94,877 and writing down allowances at 19.87% on the remaining £15,123 of his expenditure, giving him total allowances of £97,882.

If Woody incurs this expenditure between 6th and 30th April 2012, however, he will be able to claim an annual investment allowance of just £1,708, together with writing down allowances of 9.87% on the remaining £58,292 of his integral features and 19.87% on his other equipment purchases: giving him total allowances of just £17,396!

The Government claims that it wishes to make the UK tax system both simpler and fairer and yet a difference of just one day in the timing of his expenditure could cost Woody over £80,000 in lost capital allowances!

Combining that with the current top rate of combined Income Tax and National Insurance at 52%, and Woody could be up to £41,853 worse off as a result!

(See Appendix F re the writing down allowances rates used in this section.)

7.5 TIMING YOUR EXPENDITURE IN TRANSITIONAL PERIODS

Timing your expenditure carefully during and after your transitional accounting period could lead to considerable tax savings.

The restriction in the annual investment allowance for the period between the date of change and your next accounting date means that, in many cases, you will obtain very little tax relief for qualifying expenditure incurred on plant and machinery during this period.

Appendices D and E set out the maximum annual investment allowance claims for expenditure in the affected periods. If it all possible, it may make sense to ensure that these limits are not exceeded.

Where the business might potentially wish to spend in excess of these amounts, there are two basic choices:

i) Accelerate the expenditure to before the date of change. Also included in Appendices D and E are the minimum amounts which you will need to spend by 31st March 2012 (for companies) or 5th April 2012 (for other businesses) in order to be able to secure the maximum annual investment allowance for the accounting period as a whole.

ii) Defer the expenditure until your next accounting period. By deferring up to £25,000 of qualifying expenditure on plant and machinery until your next accounting period, you will be able to obtain immediate 100% tax relief on this expenditure.

Example

Inglis Limited plans to spend £120,000 on plant and machinery qualifying for the general pool during the year ending 30th June 2012. If it spends the whole amount during the period between 1st April and 30th June 2012, it will be entitled to an annual investment allowance of just £6,216 (see Appendix D) and writing down allowances at 19.51% (see Appendix F) on the remainder.

This will give the company total capital allowances for the year ending 30th June 2012 of just £28,415.

The balance of £91,585 carried forward on the company's general pool will then generate further writing down allowances of £16,485 (at 18%) in the year ending 30th June 2013, giving the company total capital allowances over the two year period of £44,900.

Instead of this, however, the company brings forward £80,000 of its expenditure to March and defers a further £25,000 to July, spending only £15,000 between 1st April and 30th June 2012.

The company will now be able to claim the maximum annual investment allowance available for the year ending 30th June 2012: £81,352 (see Appendix D). This leaves just £13,648 of its expenditure of £95,000 during the year to fall into the general pool and attract writing down allowances of £2,663 (at 19.51%).

In the following year, the company will be able to claim an annual investment allowance of £25,000 on the expenditure which it deferred until July plus a further £1,977 in writing down allowances at 18%.

In summary, the company will now be able to claim total capital allowances of £110,992 over the two year period – £66,092 more than if it had incurred all of the expenditure in the period from April to June as originally intended.

Tax Savings

By timing its qualifying expenditure on plant and machinery carefully, Inglis Limited will be able to save between £13,218 and £17,839 in Corporation Tax over a two year period.

A higher rate taxpayer sole trader undertaking similar planning could save up to £34,368 over two years (at the current maximum combined rate of Income Tax and National Insurance: 52%).

If the plant and machinery described in the example had instead been integral features or other items falling into the special rate pool then Inglis Limited would have been able to save between £16,673 and £22,444 in Corporation Tax over the same two year period. A higher rate taxpayer sole trader could save up to £43,350!

Naturally, all of this is subject to the commercial requirements of the business. Nevertheless, whilst it is seldom worth spending money just to save tax, it may often be worth spending it a little sooner or a little later!

7.6   OTHER PLANNING TECHNIQUES

If the business cannot avoid spending more on qualifying plant and machinery than the maximum annual investment allowance available for its transitional period, then it will be worth considering the other planning techniques which we looked at in Chapter 6.

The abilities to make short-life asset elections, claim enhanced capital allowances on the items described in Section 1.5, or claim the other allowances we looked at in Chapter 3 are all unaffected by the transitional rules described in this chapter, so these planning techniques could all be extremely valuable during the transitional period.

Chapter 8

Second-Hand Property

8.1 NEW RESTRICTIONS

The second major set of changes which the Government is proposing to implement with effect from April 2012 is a new regime to restrict capital allowances claims on fixtures in second-hand property.

The proposed changes will make it imperative for purchasers of qualifying property to obtain the right paperwork from sellers or other sources – on pain of losing out on most, if not all, of the capital allowances on the property which they would otherwise have been entitled to!

Purchasers will also need to meet strict new time limits for arranging this paperwork. Again, failure to do so will mean losing out on the capital allowances on their new property. As we saw in Sections 2.4 and 2.5, this may amount to a considerable sum!

The new restrictions will apply to properties purchased after:

- 31st March 2012, where the purchaser is a company, or
- 5th April 2012, in other cases

Current property owners will also need to take action to ensure that all of the qualifying plant and machinery within their properties is identified and 'pooled' for capital allowances purposes (see Section 8.8) before any sale takes place. Anyone failing to do so is likely to suffer a considerable reduction in the sale price which their property is able to command.

8.2   WHICH PROPERTIES ARE AFFECTED?

The new regime will apply to all properties used in any qualifying activity (see Section 1.2). In effect, this means that it will apply to:

- Commercial property (including offices, shops, factories, warehouses, farm buildings, etc)
- Furnished holiday lettings
- Rented residential property which has any 'communal areas' (see Section 2.10)

Properties come into the regime as soon as they are in use for a qualifying activity at any time falling on or after the commencement date, which is:

- 1st April 2012 for companies, or
- 6th April 2012 for other businesses

Hence properties which are in use in a qualifying activity at the beginning of April 2012 will generally be brought within the regime immediately.

Other properties may be brought within the regime at a later date.

Example

Marie used Seaview Cottage as a furnished holiday let until she sold it to Matthew in February 2012. Matthew used the property as a second home and did not rent it out at all. In May 2014, Matthew sold the property to Lynne.

Lynne adopted the cottage as a furnished holiday let from 1st June 2014 and this means that it entered the new regime from that date. However, as the property was not used in a qualifying activity at any earlier time after 5th April 2012, Lynne's purchase is unaffected by the new regime and she may claim capital allowances on the qualifying fixtures in the cottage without being subject to the restrictions described in this chapter.

However, when Lynne sells the property, that sale will be subject to the new regime, as will any subsequent sale where the purchaser adopts the property for use in a qualifying activity.

We will look at capital allowances claims on properties which do not fall within the new regime in Section 8.15.

8.3   WHAT ARE FIXTURES?

The new regime will apply to capital allowances claims on 'fixtures' within qualifying property purchased on or after the commencement dates set out in Section 8.2.

Existing tax legislation defines 'fixtures' as 'plant or machinery that is so installed or otherwise fixed in or to a building, or on land, as to become, in law, part of that building or land'. (This is not quite a direct quote from the legislation: I have amended it slightly for sense!)

The legislation also specifically identifies 'any boiler or water-filled radiator installed in a building as part of a space or water heating system' as being fixtures.

In effect, therefore, a 'fixture' is any asset which 'transfers with the property'. Central heating systems are, for some reason, also singled out for specific inclusion!

In short, most of the assets described in Sections 2.4 and 2.5 are likely to be regarded as 'fixtures' for the purposes of the new regime with the possible exception of some of the following items when these are not actually fixed to the building:

- Manufacturing and processing equipment
- Furniture
- Decorative assets provided for the enjoyment of the public (in hotels, restaurants, and other similar establishments)

8.4   WHICH FIXTURES ARE CAUGHT?

Having defined what constitutes a 'fixture', it is important to point out that not all qualifying fixtures will necessarily fall within the new regime.

In Section 8.2, we looked at when a property falls into the new regime.

However, the fixtures within that property only fall into the new regime when any owner from that time onwards is eligible to claim capital allowances on those fixtures.

Hence, when none of the previous owners at any time on or after the commencement dates set out in Section 8.2 were entitled to claim capital allowances on any particular 'fixture', then that fixture is not within the scope of the new regime.

The main application of this exclusion will be when the seller originally purchased the property before 6th April 2008 (or 1st April 2008 for companies). In this case, the following integral features which were already within the property before April 2008 will not usually fall within the new regime:

- Electrical lighting and power systems
- Cold water systems
- External solar shading

Note, however, that any specialised cold water, electrical or lighting systems which had previously been installed to meet the specific requirements of the trade being carried on in the property might fall within the regime.

Example

Dawson Limited bought a commercial property in 2007. In 2009, the company had the property rewired at a cost of £20,000 and this was treated as capital expenditure under the rules set out in Section 2.6.

In 2013, Dawson Limited sold the property to Morgan, a property investor. On this occasion, the £20,000 worth of rewiring is caught by the new regime but none of the other electrical, lighting or cold water systems in the property are caught (nor indeed any external solar shading which the property has).

In 2015, Morgan sells the property to Stella, another property investor. On this occasion, all of the integral features and fixtures within the property are caught by the new regime.

Another important exclusion applies where an item is sold 'not as a fixture'. For example, where a very old boiler is stripped out of a property and sold to a dealer in industrial antiques (or perhaps a scrap merchant) it would drop out of the new regime. Where the item was subsequently installed in a new property being used in a qualifying activity, it would re-enter the regime from that point onwards.

Practical Pointer

A close examination of the draft legislation appears to suggest that any fixtures purchased by the previous owner (i.e. the seller) before 24th July 1996 may not be within the scope of the new regime.

We have sought clarification from HM Revenue and Customs on this point but, at the time of writing, we are yet to receive a satisfactory reply. As soon as we do receive any clarification, we will post the answer to this point at: www.taxcafe.co.uk/fixturesconfirmation.html

8.5   FIXTURES OUTSIDE THE REGIME

Where a purchaser acquires a property with qualifying fixtures which do not fall within the new regime due to any of the exclusions described in Section 8.4, they may claim capital allowances on those fixtures based on a reasonable allocation of the purchase price of the property.

Hence, in the example in Section 8.4, when Morgan purchased the commercial property from Dawson Limited, she would have been able to claim capital allowances on the cold water system, and any part of the electrical and lighting systems which predated the rewiring carried out in 2009, based on a reasonable allocation of the purchase price of the property and without any regard to the requirements under the new regime.

8.6   NEW REGIME REQUIREMENTS

A purchaser of second-hand property which falls within the regime (see Section 8.2) who wishes to claim capital allowances on fixtures within the property which fall within the regime (see Section 8.4) must satisfy:

i)   The 'Pooling Requirement', and
ii) Either:
      a.   The 'Fixed Value Requirement', or
      b.   The 'Disposal Value Statement Requirement'

We will look at each of these requirements in detail in Sections 8.8 to 8.10.

However, it is worth noting that the 'Pooling Requirement' does not apply to property purchases taking place during the transitional period ending on:

- 31st March 2014 where the purchaser is a company, or
- 5th April 2014 for other businesses

As we will see in later sections, 'satisfying' the requirements of the new regime will usually necessitate more action by the seller than the purchaser, but it is the purchaser who must 'satisfy' them by: ensuring that the requisite action does take place, obtaining the appropriate evidence, and providing it to HM Revenue and Customs where required.

Furthermore, it is in the purchaser's interests to make sure that the requirements are satisfied, as they are the ones who will lose out on the capital allowances which they are due otherwise!

8.7   THE PAST OWNER

Before we look at the detailed requirements under the new regime, I need to define an important term: the 'past owner'.

For the purposes of the new capital allowances regime for second-hand property, the 'past owner' will usually mean the seller of the property. However, where the seller was not carrying on a qualifying activity, the 'past owner' for this purpose will be the most recent owner who was using the property for a qualifying activity at any time on or after the commencement dates given in Section 8.2.

If no owner has used the property in a qualifying activity since the relevant commencement date, the regime simply does not apply.

8.8 THE POOLING REQUIREMENT

The 'pooling requirement' quite simply means that the past owner must have 'claimed' capital allowances on the fixtures.

When I say that the past owner must have 'claimed' capital allowances, they are only required to have added the relevant fixtures to their general pool or special rate pool, as appropriate. They do not need to have actually 'claimed' the allowances due to them, so any 'disclaimer' (see Section 4.5) will not affect the purchaser's position.

Claiming the annual investment allowance or first year allowances on the fixtures also means that they have been added to a pool for this purpose.

More importantly, however, the fact that the past owner has 'claimed' capital allowances by adding the cost of the fixtures to one of their pools means that they must deduct a suitable value from one or both of the pools when they sell the property.

The past owner may 'claim' the relevant capital allowances in any accounting period commencing on or before the date they sell the property.

Renovated Property

The pooling requirement is also met where the past owner has claimed the Business Premises Renovation Allowance on the cost of the fixtures but has not yet claimed the allowance in full (see Section 3.1).

8.9 THE FIXED VALUE REQUIREMENT

As we saw in Section 8.6, the purchaser must meet either the 'fixed value requirement' or the 'disposal value statement requirement'.

This is not a question of choice, however. The question of which of these two requirements applies is dependent on the circumstances surrounding the past owner's disposal of the property.

The fixed value requirement will usually apply in most cases, including where the past owner:

i)   Sells the property (except where it is sold at less than market value to a purchaser who does not use it in a qualifying activity),

ii) Grants a long lease in the property and charges a lease premium (see Section 2.9), and then jointly elects with the lessee that the lessee should be treated as the owner of the fixtures for capital allowances purposes

iii) Ceases the qualifying activity which the property was being used in and then sells the property immediately afterwards

In short, this requirement will apply to most property purchases falling within the new regime.

So What Is The Requirement?

The fixed value requirement is that the past owner and the purchaser must agree a fixed value for the qualifying fixtures within the property by making a joint election.

The election will only cover the assets on which the past owner was entitled to claim capital allowances (see Section 8.4).

The election is made under Section 198 of the Capital Allowances Act 2001. It is thus commonly referred to as a 'Section 198 Election'.

The normal time limit for a Section 198 Election is two years from the date of purchase of the property. The time limit is only extended under the circumstances described below.

The value fixed under a Section 198 Election cannot exceed the past owner's original cost for the fixtures. Subject to this, however, it can be as low as the purchaser is willing to accept.

Where the past owner had themselves been party to a Section 198 Election with the previous owner before them, this will have fixed their original cost for capital allowances purposes and will thus form the new maximum for the current election. In this way, the values of historic fixtures are prevented from ever being increased under new ownership in the future.

What If You Cannot Agree A Value?

If the parties cannot agree a value for the qualifying fixtures within the property, then either party may apply to the tax tribunal (normally the First Tier Tax Tribunal) to determine a value.

The application to the tribunal must be made within two years from the date of purchase of the property.

If an application has been made within the requisite time limit, but the parties are subsequently able to reach an agreement before the tribunal has reached a decision, then they may make a Section 198 Election at any time before the tribunal hands down its determination.

Once the tribunal reaches a determination, however, the value determined by the tribunal is then binding on both parties.

What Happens Next?

Once a value has been fixed, either by way of a Section 198 Election, or a tribunal determination, the past owner must use that value as the disposal value for the fixtures in the property in their capital allowances computation.

The purchaser must use the same value as the purchase price of the fixtures in their capital allowances computation. Occasionally, as explained in Section 8.5, they may also be able to make further claims on assets outside the regime.

8.10 THE DISPOSAL VALUE STATEMENT REQUIREMENT

The disposal value statement requirement applies if the past owner:

i) Sold the property at less than market value to a person who did not use it in a qualifying activity, or
ii) Ceased to own the fixtures in the property under other circumstances not already covered under (i) above or items (i) to (iii) in Section 8.9 above

The requirement is that the past owner must make a written statement of the disposal value of the fixtures in the property used for the purposes of their capital allowances computations. As with a Section 198 Election, this value cannot exceed the past owner's original cost for the fixtures.

The statement must be made in writing within two years of the date that the past owner ceases to own the property, or to be deemed to own the fixtures within it.

The purchaser of the property can only claim capital allowances on the fixtures in the property if they obtain a copy of the disposal value statement. They may then claim capital allowances on the relevant disposal value.

As usual, further claims may be possible where there are additional fixtures in the property outside the new regime, as discussed in Section 8.5.

8.11 FURTHER REQUIREMENTS

In the tax return covering the accounting period in which the property is purchased, the purchaser will be required to show why the fixed value requirement applies, or why the disposal value statement requirement applies (as appropriate), and how the relevant requirement has been met.

If requested by HM Revenue and Customs, the purchaser will also need to provide a copy of the relevant Section 198 Election, tribunal decision, or disposal value statement, as appropriate.

8.12 CHANGE OF USE

Where, at any time after the relevant commencement date given in Section 8.2, the owner of a property changes its use from one qualifying activity to another (see Section 1.2), or ceases to use it in a qualifying activity and then later re-adopts it for the same qualifying activity, or another one, the property will fall into the new regime.

The property owner will then need to meet the requirements of the new regime in order to claim any capital allowances on the fixtures in the property for the purposes of their new qualifying activity.

The owner will be regarded as being both the 'past owner' and the purchaser for this purpose.

In most cases, this means that the owner will need to produce a disposal value statement, as described in Section 8.10. From April 2014, it will also mean that they will only be able to claim capital allowances on fixtures in their new qualifying activity if they also claimed capital allowances on those same fixtures in their old qualifying activity.

8.13 ACTION FOR PURCHASERS

Ideally, anyone purchasing qualifying property from April 2012 onwards, from a seller who is using it in a qualifying activity, should negotiate a suitable value for the qualifying fixtures and then enter a Section 198 Election with the seller.

Such negotiations are best carried out before the purchase is completed!

If agreement cannot be reached on a suitable value for the fixtures then you have the choice of buying a different property or applying to the tribunal for a determination.

For purchases from April 2014 onwards, you will also need to ensure that the seller has 'claimed' all the capital allowances due on fixtures within the property (see Section 8.8). The seller can still do this in any accounting period beginning on or before the date of the sale but, again, it is best to ensure that this happens before the sale is completed.

Where a property is not currently being used in a qualifying activity, you will need to research its history to see whether it falls within the new regime. If it does, you will need to obtain suitable documentation to support any capital allowances claim. If you cannot, you may not be entitled to any capital allowances on the property!

Finally, always remember that it is worth considering whether there might be any additional fixtures within the property which are not covered by the new regime, especially cold water, electrical and lighting systems in properties which the seller acquired before April 2008.

8.14 ACTION FOR CURRENT OWNERS

It is well known that there are millions of pounds worth of unclaimed capital allowances on fixtures within:

- Commercial property
- Furnished holiday lettings
- Communal areas within rented residential property

Owners of these properties may be able to make considerable savings by carrying out a detailed review of their properties to see what additional allowances may be available on the items described in Sections 2.4 and 2.5.

This was always the case but, due to the 'pooling requirement' explained in Section 8.8, it may soon be difficult to sell these properties if you have not maximised your potential capital allowances claims. At best, you may have to offer significant discounts on the sale price!

Furthermore, whilst the pooling requirement only applies to purchases from April 2014 onwards, potential purchasers are likely to begin pressurising sellers to agree higher values for qualifying fixtures from April 2012. The only way to respond without incurring additional tax charges will again be to maximise your own capital allowances claims before sales take place.

In short, current property owners need to maximise their capital allowances claims as soon as possible.

8.15 PURCHASES OUTSIDE THE REGIME

For purchases taking place before the commencement dates given in Section 8.2, and other purchases falling outside the new regime (also explained in Section 8.2), purchasers may either:

- Enter a Section 198 Election with the seller, or
- Allocate a reasonable proportion of the purchase price to the qualifying fixtures within the property

Section 198 Elections are not compulsory at present but are still a useful way to obtain an agreed value which is used consistently by both parties. Generally, however, sellers tend to attempt to put extremely low values in the elections which is clearly disadvantageous to purchasers.

Although Section 198 Elections are currently optional, where they are used, they are binding on both parties. Note, however, that they only fix the value for the fixtures on which the seller has previously claimed capital allowances. The purchaser may still make additional claims on any further qualifying items on a reasonable basis.

Without a Section 198 Election, a purchaser may currently make a capital allowances claim on a reasonable proportion of the property's purchase price. The amount claimed should, however:

- Not exceed the seller's original cost for the qualifying fixtures, and
- Be the same as the disposal value used by the seller

Well, that's the theory at least. In practice, in the absence of a Section 198 Election, it is often difficult for a purchaser to ensure that these requirements are met. HM Revenue and Customs also has difficulty in overturning any capital allowances claims which, although reasonable, do not meet these requirements.

Only a Section 198 Election is binding on a purchaser. Allocations made in a sale agreement may be persuasive regarding what is reasonable, but they are not binding.

Chapter 9

Houses in Multiple Occupation

9.1 BACKGROUND

As explained in Section 2.10, residential landlords are able to claim capital allowances on qualifying integral features, fixtures and other assets within 'communal areas' which do not lie within a rented 'dwelling house'.

The most obvious example of this is in the case of a property which is divided into self-contained flats. We will see an example of this type in Section 9.2.

However, there has been a great deal of fuss over the last couple of years over the question of just how far the idea of 'communal areas' could be pushed.

At one point, some people seemed to be suggesting that practically any landlord with a 'house in multiple occupation' ('HMO') was entitled to a massive claim and a large tax refund from HM Revenue and Customs. It would have been nice if this were true but the reality, not surprisingly, is that this apparent windfall was only ever going to be available to a few property investors.

Nonetheless, for landlords who happen to fall within the appropriate criteria, significant capital allowances claims and tax refunds may still be possible!

9.2 DWELLING HOUSES

As explained in Chapter 2, tax legislation specifically prohibits landlords from claiming capital allowances on expenditure within a rented 'dwelling-house' (except qualifying furnished holiday lets).

Despite this, it is well established that the communal areas in a block of flats are not part of a 'dwelling-house'. In fact, where any building comprises 'self-contained' flats, the areas outside the flats are not within a dwelling-house and appropriate capital allowances may be claimed.

Example

In May 2012, Ernie buys a large townhouse and converts it into six bedsits. He also installs a utility room in the basement.

Each of the bedsits is a 'dwelling-house' and the remainder of the property lying outside them is eligible for capital allowances.

Ernie can therefore claim immediate tax relief for up to £25,000 of expenditure on the 'integral features' (see Section 2.5) outside the bedsits, as well as all of the equipment in the utility room.

So there are indeed some HMO landlords who could benefit from capital allowances claims and, if they haven't claimed already, could get a substantial refund from HM Revenue and Customs.

In a case like Ernie's, where capital allowances can be claimed, he will need to apportion the cost of items like central heating, which run through all parts of the building, between the qualifying (communal) and non-qualifying (private) areas. Where the non-qualifying element amounts to no more than 25%, however, the entire cost may then be claimed.

9.3 BRIEF CONFUSION

The idea of what constituted a 'dwelling-house' and what was 'communal space' was reasonably well understood until December 2008 when HM Revenue and Customs issued a new brief on the subject (Brief 66/08).

HM Revenue and Customs intended Brief 66/08 as an update to add further clarification to their existing guidance on the question of what constituted a 'dwelling-house' for capital allowances purposes. In particular, the brief was aimed at clarifying the position for student accommodation owned by private property investors.

The type of property discussed in the brief is sometimes known as 'cluster flats'. These are typically used for student accommodation and consist of en-suite study bedrooms 'clustered' in groups of around six to ten which, together with a shared kitchen/dining area and living room, comprise a 'flat'. The flats are then usually housed in blocks, with one or two such flats on each floor.

In Brief 66/08, HM Revenue and Customs stated that it accepted that each bedroom within this type of property was a separate dwelling-house, so that capital allowances could be claimed on all the qualifying expenditure within the property outside the bedrooms.

The brief also stated that the same treatment would be extended to 'other similar properties in multiple occupation, such as key-worker accommodation'.

9.4 BRIEF REACTION

At this point, some people became very excited. They interpreted Brief 66/08 to mean that the communal areas in almost any HMO were eligible for capital allowances and started aggressively marketing packages aimed at encouraging landlords and property investors to make claims on this basis.

The difficulty following Brief 66/08 was in understanding exactly where the boundary between private and communal space was supposed to lie, especially in the more conventional HMO, where the property is shared more extensively than in Ernie's case (see Section 9.2).

Example

Eric rents a house to three unrelated young professionals. Each tenant has their own bedroom but they all share a bathroom, kitchen and living room.

The suggestion from some people was that each tenant's bedroom in a case like this should be regarded as a dwelling-house and the remainder of the property was therefore communal space. By implication, the landlord could therefore claim capital allowances on all furniture, equipment and 'integral features' throughout the entire property except for the bedrooms. As you can imagine, this would amount to a substantial claim.

Personally, I was never comfortable with this view. To me, the tenants in a typical HMO of this nature clearly live as a single household and the entire property is therefore a single dwelling-house.

Any other interpretation seemed to me to be going way beyond what was intended by Brief 66/08 which was clearly aimed at the particular circumstances of students and key-workers in bespoke accommodation designed for that purpose.

9.5   LATEST GUIDANCE

Eventually, HM Revenue and Customs woke up to the fact that Brief 66/08 was being interpreted rather more widely than intended. In October 2010, it issued further revised guidance in the form of Brief 45/10. For full text see:

www.hmrc.gov.uk/briefs/income-tax/brief4510.htm

The main change between Brief 66/08 and Brief 45/10 is that HM Revenue and Customs now interprets the term 'dwelling-house' to mean a building, or part of a building, which has 'the facilities required for day-to-day private domestic existence'.

In itself, this seems like a reasonably sensible definition and this latest change of approach should make absolutely no difference to the vast majority of landlords and property investors.

If we go back to our two earlier examples, Ernie (who rents out self-contained bedsits – see Section 9.2) will continue to be eligible for capital allowances on all the qualifying expenditure within the communal areas in his property, whereas Eric (who rents a house to three tenants who each have private bedrooms but share all other facilities – see Section 9.4) will not be eligible for any capital allowances.

Brief 45/10 also goes on to revisit the position for 'cluster flats' (see Section 9.3). Here HM Revenue and Customs has changed its view and is now saying that each 'flat' must be regarded as a dwelling-house, leaving just the stairwell and other areas outside the 'flats' (e.g. lifts, boiler room, air-conditioning units, etc) eligible for capital allowances on qualifying expenditure.

9.6   CLAIMS OPPORTUNITY

Despite having now published the more restrictive guidance in Brief 45/10, HM Revenue and Customs will accept claims based on their earlier guidance in Brief 66/08 where the qualifying expenditure took place between 29th December 2008 and 21st October 2010, or where the relevant tax return was submitted before 22nd October 2010.

For any landlords or property investors affected by the change between Brief 66/08 and Brief 45/10 there is an opportunity to make additional capital allowances claims on expenditure incurred between December 2008 and October 2010.

Remember that claims for past expenditure may continue to be made using the procedures set out in Sections 4.3 and 4.4.

9.7   MIDDLE GROUND

The position for both Eric and Ernie (see Sections 9.4 and 9.2 respectively) now seems fairly clear: Ernie can claim some capital allowances on his property, Eric cannot. In my view, this has always been the case.

There will be some landlords for whom the position is less clear, however, and for whom the difference between Brief 66/08 and Brief 45/10 may be critical.

Example

Angela rents out a property with private bedrooms which each have an en suite toilet and shower room, a kitchenette and a small dining area. The property also has a communal living room, bathroom and utility room.

Under the guidance set out in Brief 66/08, Angela would seem to have a good case for saying that the en suite bedrooms form dwelling-houses in their own right and that she should therefore be entitled to claim capital allowances on qualifying expenditure throughout the rest of the property.

There is therefore a fair chance that HM Revenue and Customs would accept such a claim where the relevant expenditure was incurred between 29th December 2008 and 21st October 2010.

But if Angela does not meet these criteria then HM Revenue and Customs is now saying that she would need to meet the conditions set out in Brief 45/10. In other words, she would only be able to claim capital allowances if the bedrooms in her property have 'the facilities required for day-to-day private domestic existence'.

This is more doubtful and clearly open to debate in this particular case. Sadly, it is too soon to say exactly how HM Revenue and Customs will apply Brief 45/10 in practice and whether it might therefore attempt to deny any capital allowances claim which Angela makes.

9.8   GUIDANCE VERSUS LAW

HM Revenue and Customs' guidance can be very useful, but it is important to remember that it is not the law: only Parliament and the Courts can set the law!

Both Brief 66/08 and Brief 45/10 merely give us HM Revenue and Customs' opinion at different points in time. The actual law relating to this issue has remained unchanged. Where justified, it is still possible to make a claim on general principles, even when this is contrary to HM Revenue and Customs' guidance.

This is where the waters get very muddy, however, because the relevant tax legislation does not actually define a 'dwelling-house'. This means that we must look to see what the term's general, everyday, or common-sense meaning is. Until a High Court judge tells us what they think it means, anyway.

Nevertheless, if a claim is justified under basic principles, and there is enough at stake, no one should be put off just by HM Revenue and Customs' opinion.

9.9 CONCLUSION

Where a property is made up of self-contained flats, a capital allowances claim on qualifying expenditure within communal areas will generally be justified.

For 'cluster flats' (see Section 9.3) and other properties with significant facilities in tenants' bedrooms, there is greater scope to make claims in respect of expenditure incurred between 29th December 2008 and 21st October 2010.

In other cases, the grounds for claims range from being uncertain to highly doubtful. In borderline cases (again, where there are significant facilities in tenants' bedrooms), it could sometimes be worth making a claim, but there may be a risk attached.

Appendix A

UK Tax Rates and Allowances: 2010/11 to 2012/13

	Rates	2010/11 £	2011/12 £	2012/13 £
Income Tax				
Personal allowance		6,475	7,475	8,105
Basic rate band	20%	37,400	35,000	34,370
Higher rate/Threshold	40%	43,875	42,475	42,475
Personal allowance withdrawal				
Effective rate/From	60%	100,000	100,000	100,000
To		112,950	114,950	116,210
Super tax rate/Threshold	50%	150,000	150,000	150,000
Starting rate band applying to interest and other savings income only				
	10%	2,440	2,560	2,710
National Insurance				
Class 1 – Primary		11%	12%	12%
Class 4		8%	9%	9%
Primary threshold		5,715	7,225	7,605
Upper earnings limit		43,875	42,475	42,475
Additional Rate		1%	2%	2%
Class 1 – Secondary		12.8%	13.8%	13.8%
Secondary threshold		5,715	7,075	7,488
Class 2 – per week		2.40	2.50	2.65
Small earnings exception		5,075	5,315	5,595
Class 3 – per week		12.05	12.60	13.25
Pension Contributions				
Annual allowance		255,000	50,000	50,000
Lifetime allowance		1.8m	1.8m	1.5m
Capital Gains Tax				
Annual exemption		10,100	10,600	10,600
Basic rate		18%	18%	18%
Higher rate		28% (1)	28%	28%
Entrepreneurs' relief:				
Lifetime limit		2m/5m (1)	10m	10m
Rate of relief/Tax rate		4/9ths/10%(1)	10%	10%
Inheritance Tax				
Nil Rate Band		325,000	325,000	325,000
Annual Exemption		3,000	3,000	3,000

Age-related Allowances, etc.

Age allowance: 65-74	9,490	9,940	10,500
Age allowance: 75 and over	9,640	10,090	10,660
MCA: born before 6/4/1935 (2)	6,965	7,295	7,705
MCA minimum	2,670	2,800	2,960
Income limit	22,900	24,000	25,400
Blind Person's Allowance	1,890	1,980	2,100

Notes

1. Capital Gains Tax changes were introduced with effect from 23ʳ June 2010.
2. The Married Couples Allowance, 'MCA', is given at a rate of 10%.

The European Union &
The European Economic Area

The European Union

The 27 member states of the European Union are:

Austria	admitted 1st January 1995
Belgium	founding member
Bulgaria	admitted 1st January 2007
Cyprus	admitted 1st May 2004
Czech Republic	admitted 1st May 2004
Denmark	admitted 1st January 1973
Estonia	admitted 1st May 2004
Finland	admitted 1st January 1995
France	founding member
Germany	founding member
Greece	admitted 1st January 1981
Hungary	admitted 1st May 2004
Irish Republic	admitted 1st January 1973
Italy	founding member
Latvia	admitted 1st May 2004
Lithuania	admitted 1st May 2004
Luxembourg	founding member
Malta	admitted 1st May 2004
Netherlands	founding member
Poland	admitted 1st May 2004
Portugal	admitted 1st January 1986
Romania	admitted 1st January 2007
Slovakia	admitted 1st May 2004
Slovenia	admitted 1st May 2004
Spain	admitted 1st January 1986
Sweden	admitted 1st January 1995
United Kingdom	admitted 1st January 1973

Any rights which citizens of countries admitted on 1st May 2004 or 1st January 2007 have under UK tax law commence on the date that their country was admitted to membership.

The European Economic Area comprises the 27 member states of the European Union plus Iceland, Liechtenstein and Norway.

Appendix C

Connected Persons

The definition of 'connected persons' differs slightly from one area of UK tax law to another. Generally, however, an individual's connected persons include the following:

i) Their husband, wife or civil partner
ii) The following relatives:
  o Mother, father or remoter ancestor
  o Son, daughter or remoter descendant
  o Brother or sister

iii) Relatives under (ii) above of the individual's spouse or civil partner
iv) Spouses or civil partners of the individual's relatives under (ii) above
v) The individual's business partners
vi) Companies under the control of the individual or of any of their relatives under (i) to (iv) above
vii) Trusts where the individual, or any of their relatives under (i) to (iv) above, is a beneficiary

Appendix D

Annual Investment Allowance for Companies

The maximum annual investment allowances for twelve month company accounting periods affected by the transitional rules discussed in Chapter 7 are set out below.

The first column gives the maximum annual investment allowance ('AIA') for the whole accounting period.

The second column gives the maximum annual investment allowance for the period from 1st April 2012 to the end of the accounting period.

The third column indicates the minimum amount of qualifying expenditure which needs to be incurred between the start of the accounting period and 31st March 2012 in order for the company to be able to obtain the maximum annual investment allowance for the whole accounting period.

Year ended	Max AIA for whole year	Max AIA after 31/3/2012	Min spend by 31/3/2012 to get max relief
30-Apr-2012	£93,852	£2,049	£91,803
31-May-2012	£87,500	£4,167	£83,333
30-Jun-2012	£81,352	£6,216	£75,137
31-Jul-2012	£75,000	£8,333	£66,667
31-Aug-2012	£68,648	£10,451	£58,197
30-Sep-2012	£62,500	£12,500	£50,000
31-Oct-2012	£56,148	£14,617	£41,530
30-Nov-2012	£50,000	£16,667	£33,333
31-Dec-2012	£43,648	£18,784	£24,863
31-Jan-2013	£37,295	£20,902	£16,393
28-Feb-2013	£31,557	£22,814	£8,743

Appendix E

Annual Investment Allowance for Other Businesses

The maximum annual investment allowances for twelve month accounting periods of businesses (other than companies) affected by the transitional rules discussed in Chapter 7 are set out below.

The first column gives the maximum annual investment allowance ('AIA') for the whole accounting period.

The second column gives the maximum annual investment allowance for the period from 6th April 2012 to the end of the accounting period.

The third column indicates the minimum amount of qualifying expenditure which needs to be incurred between the start of the accounting period and 5th April 2012 in order for the company to be able to obtain the maximum annual investment allowance for the whole accounting period.

Year ended	Max AIA for whole year	Max AIA after 5/4/2012	Min spend by 5/4/2012 to get max relief
30-Apr-2012	£94,877	£1,708	£93,169
31-May-2012	£88,525	£3,825	£84,699
30-Jun-2012	£82,377	£5,874	£76,503
31-Jul-2012	£76,025	£7,992	£68,033
31-Aug-2012	£69,672	£10,109	£59,563
30-Sep-2012	£63,525	£12,158	£51,366
31-Oct-2012	£57,172	£14,276	£42,896
30-Nov-2012	£51,025	£16,325	£34,699
31-Dec-2012	£44,672	£18,443	£26,230
31-Jan-2013	£38,320	£20,560	£17,760
28-Feb-2013	£32,582	£22,473	£10,109
31-Mar-2013	£26,027	£24,658	£1,370

Appendix F

Writing Down Allowances

The rates of writing down allowances applying to twelve month accounting periods affected by the transitional rules discussed in Chapter 7 are set out below.

Year ended	Companies		Other Businesses	
	General Pool	Special Rate Pool	General Pool	Special Rate Pool
30-Apr-2012	19.84%	9.84%	19.87%	9.87%
31-May-2012	19.67%	9.67%	19.70%	9.70%
30-Jun-2012	19.51%	9.51%	19.54%	9.54%
31-Jul-2012	19.34%	9.34%	19.37%	9.37%
31-Aug-2012	19.17%	9.17%	19.20%	9.20%
30-Sep-2012	19.00%	9.00%	19.03%	9.03%
31-Oct-2012	18.84%	8.84%	18.86%	8.86%
30-Nov-2012	18.67%	8.67%	18.70%	8.70%
31-Dec-2012	18.50%	8.50%	18.53%	8.53%
31-Jan-2013	18.33%	8.33%	18.36%	8.36%
28-Feb-2013	18.18%	8.18%	18.21%	8.21%
31-Mar-2013	18.00%	8.00%	18.03%	8.03%

The rate applying to the general pool also applies to cars with CO_2 emissions of over 110g/km but not more than 160g/km.

The rate applying to the special rate pool also applies to cars with CO_2 emissions of more than 160g/km.

Lightning Source UK Ltd.
Milton Keynes UK
UKOW030905210512

192975UK00002B/5/P